# MY B

## WATCHING JOURNAL

## THIS BOOK BELONGS TO:

# DO YOU LIKE BUGS AND INSECTS? CHECK OUT OUR MY BUG LOG BOOK!

## SEE MORE OF OUR PRODUCTS

# BIRD WATCHING LOG

| DATE: | TIME: ☐ AM ☐ PM |
|---|---|
| SEASON: | HABITAT: |
| LOCATION: | GPS: |
| WEATHER: | TEMPERATURE: |
| BIRD NAME: | BIRD TYPE: |

| BEAK SHAPE | TAIL | BIRD'S LOCATION |
|---|---|---|
| ☐ CONE | ☐ SHORT | ☐ GROUND |
| ☐ HOOKED | ☐ LONG | ☐ TREE |
| ☐ LONG-THIN | ☐ WIDE | ☐ BUSH |
| ☐ SHORT-POINTED | ☐ THIN | ☐ FEEDER |
| ☐ FLAT-WIDE | ☐ FLUFFY | ☐ FENCE |

COLOURS AND MARKINGS:

| BIRD'S ACTIONS: | DID THE BIRD SING?: ☐ YES ☐ NO |
|---|---|

## PHOTO/SKETCH

NOTES:

# BIRD WATCHING LOG

| DATE: | TIME: ☐ AM ☐ PM |
|---|---|
| SEASON: | HABITAT: |
| LOCATION: | GPS: |
| WEATHER: | TEMPERATURE: |
| BIRD NAME: | BIRD TYPE: |

| BEAK SHAPE | TAIL | BIRD'S LOCATION |
|---|---|---|
| ☐ CONE | ☐ SHORT | ☐ GROUND |
| ☐ HOOKED | ☐ LONG | ☐ TREE |
| ☐ LONG-THIN | ☐ WIDE | ☐ BUSH |
| ☐ SHORT-POINTED | ☐ THIN | ☐ FEEDER |
| ☐ FLAT-WIDE | ☐ FLUFFY | ☐ FENCE |

COLOURS AND MARKINGS:

| BIRD'S ACTIONS: | DID THE BIRD SING?:<br>☐ YES   ☐ NO |
|---|---|

## PHOTO/SKETCH

NOTES:

# BIRD WATCHING LOG

| DATE: | TIME: ☐ AM ☐ PM |
|---|---|
| SEASON: | HABITAT: |
| LOCATION: | GPS: |
| WEATHER: | TEMPERATURE: |
| BIRD NAME: | BIRD TYPE: |

| BEAK SHAPE | TAIL | BIRD'S LOCATION |
|---|---|---|
| ☐ CONE | ☐ SHORT | ☐ GROUND |
| ☐ HOOKED | ☐ LONG | ☐ TREE |
| ☐ LONG-THIN | ☐ WIDE | ☐ BUSH |
| ☐ SHORT-POINTED | ☐ THIN | ☐ FEEDER |
| ☐ FLAT-WIDE | ☐ FLUFFY | ☐ FENCE |

COLOURS AND MARKINGS:

| BIRD'S ACTIONS: | DID THE BIRD SING?: ☐ YES   ☐ NO |
|---|---|

## PHOTO/SKETCH

NOTES:

# BIRD WATCHING LOG

| DATE: | TIME: ☐ AM ☐ PM |
|---|---|
| SEASON: | HABITAT: |
| LOCATION: | GPS: |
| WEATHER: | TEMPERATURE: |
| BIRD NAME: | BIRD TYPE: |

| BEAK SHAPE | TAIL | BIRD'S LOCATION |
|---|---|---|
| ☐ CONE | ☐ SHORT | ☐ GROUND |
| ☐ HOOKED | ☐ LONG | ☐ TREE |
| ☐ LONG-THIN | ☐ WIDE | ☐ BUSH |
| ☐ SHORT-POINTED | ☐ THIN | ☐ FEEDER |
| ☐ FLAT-WIDE | ☐ FLUFFY | ☐ FENCE |

COLOURS AND MARKINGS:

| BIRD'S ACTIONS: | DID THE BIRD SING?:<br>☐ YES   ☐ NO |
|---|---|

## PHOTO/SKETCH

NOTES:

# BIRD WATCHING LOG

| DATE: | TIME: ☐ AM ☐ PM |
|---|---|
| SEASON: | HABITAT: |
| LOCATION: | GPS: |
| WEATHER: | TEMPERATURE: |
| BIRD NAME: | BIRD TYPE: |

| BEAK SHAPE | TAIL | BIRD'S LOCATION |
|---|---|---|
| ☐ CONE | ☐ SHORT | ☐ GROUND |
| ☐ HOOKED | ☐ LONG | ☐ TREE |
| ☐ LONG-THIN | ☐ WIDE | ☐ BUSH |
| ☐ SHORT-POINTED | ☐ THIN | ☐ FEEDER |
| ☐ FLAT-WIDE | ☐ FLUFFY | ☐ FENCE |

COLOURS AND MARKINGS:

| BIRD'S ACTIONS: | DID THE BIRD SING?: ☐ YES ☐ NO |
|---|---|

## PHOTO/SKETCH

NOTES:

# BIRD WATCHING LOG

| DATE: | TIME: ☐ AM ☐ PM |
|---|---|
| SEASON: | HABITAT: |
| LOCATION: | GPS: |
| WEATHER: | TEMPERATURE: |
| BIRD NAME: | BIRD TYPE: |

| BEAK SHAPE | TAIL | BIRD'S LOCATION |
|---|---|---|
| ☐ CONE | ☐ SHORT | ☐ GROUND |
| ☐ HOOKED | ☐ LONG | ☐ TREE |
| ☐ LONG-THIN | ☐ WIDE | ☐ BUSH |
| ☐ SHORT-POINTED | ☐ THIN | ☐ FEEDER |
| ☐ FLAT-WIDE | ☐ FLUFFY | ☐ FENCE |

COLOURS AND MARKINGS:

| BIRD'S ACTIONS: | DID THE BIRD SING?:<br>☐ YES   ☐ NO |
|---|---|

PHOTO/SKETCH

NOTES:

# BIRD WATCHING LOG

| DATE: | TIME: ☐ AM ☐ PM |
|---|---|
| SEASON: | HABITAT: |
| LOCATION: | GPS: |
| WEATHER: | TEMPERATURE: |
| BIRD NAME: | BIRD TYPE: |

| BEAK SHAPE | TAIL | BIRD'S LOCATION |
|---|---|---|
| ☐ CONE | ☐ SHORT | ☐ GROUND |
| ☐ HOOKED | ☐ LONG | ☐ TREE |
| ☐ LONG-THIN | ☐ WIDE | ☐ BUSH |
| ☐ SHORT-POINTED | ☐ THIN | ☐ FEEDER |
| ☐ FLAT-WIDE | ☐ FLUFFY | ☐ FENCE |

COLOURS AND MARKINGS:

| BIRD'S ACTIONS: | DID THE BIRD SING?: ☐ YES ☐ NO |
|---|---|

## PHOTO/SKETCH

NOTES:

# BIRD WATCHING LOG

| DATE: | TIME: ☐ AM ☐ PM |
|---|---|
| SEASON: | HABITAT: |
| LOCATION: | GPS: |
| WEATHER: | TEMPERATURE: |
| BIRD NAME: | BIRD TYPE: |

| BEAK SHAPE | TAIL | BIRD'S LOCATION |
|---|---|---|
| ☐ CONE | ☐ SHORT | ☐ GROUND |
| ☐ HOOKED | ☐ LONG | ☐ TREE |
| ☐ LONG-THIN | ☐ WIDE | ☐ BUSH |
| ☐ SHORT-POINTED | ☐ THIN | ☐ FEEDER |
| ☐ FLAT-WIDE | ☐ FLUFFY | ☐ FENCE |

COLOURS AND MARKINGS:

| BIRD'S ACTIONS: | DID THE BIRD SING?:<br>☐ YES  ☐ NO |
|---|---|

## PHOTO/SKETCH

NOTES:

# BIRD WATCHING LOG

| DATE: | TIME: ☐ AM ☐ PM |
|---|---|
| SEASON: | HABITAT: |
| LOCATION: | GPS: |
| WEATHER: | TEMPERATURE: |
| BIRD NAME: | BIRD TYPE: |

| BEAK SHAPE | TAIL | BIRD'S LOCATION |
|---|---|---|
| ☐ CONE | ☐ SHORT | ☐ GROUND |
| ☐ HOOKED | ☐ LONG | ☐ TREE |
| ☐ LONG-THIN | ☐ WIDE | ☐ BUSH |
| ☐ SHORT-POINTED | ☐ THIN | ☐ FEEDER |
| ☐ FLAT-WIDE | ☐ FLUFFY | ☐ FENCE |

COLOURS AND MARKINGS:

| BIRD'S ACTIONS: | DID THE BIRD SING?: ☐ YES ☐ NO |
|---|---|

## PHOTO/SKETCH

NOTES:

# BIRD WATCHING LOG

| DATE: | TIME: ☐ AM ☐ PM |
|---|---|
| SEASON: | HABITAT: |
| LOCATION: | GPS: |
| WEATHER: | TEMPERATURE: |
| BIRD NAME: | BIRD TYPE: |

| BEAK SHAPE | TAIL | BIRD'S LOCATION |
|---|---|---|
| ☐ CONE | ☐ SHORT | ☐ GROUND |
| ☐ HOOKED | ☐ LONG | ☐ TREE |
| ☐ LONG-THIN | ☐ WIDE | ☐ BUSH |
| ☐ SHORT-POINTED | ☐ THIN | ☐ FEEDER |
| ☐ FLAT-WIDE | ☐ FLUFFY | ☐ FENCE |

COLOURS AND MARKINGS:

| BIRD'S ACTIONS: | DID THE BIRD SING?: <br> ☐ YES ☐ NO |
|---|---|

### PHOTO/SKETCH

NOTES:

# BIRD WATCHING LOG

| DATE: | TIME: ☐ AM ☐ PM |
|---|---|
| SEASON: | HABITAT: |
| LOCATION: | GPS: |
| WEATHER: | TEMPERATURE: |
| BIRD NAME: | BIRD TYPE: |

| BEAK SHAPE | TAIL | BIRD'S LOCATION |
|---|---|---|
| ☐ CONE | ☐ SHORT | ☐ GROUND |
| ☐ HOOKED | ☐ LONG | ☐ TREE |
| ☐ LONG-THIN | ☐ WIDE | ☐ BUSH |
| ☐ SHORT-POINTED | ☐ THIN | ☐ FEEDER |
| ☐ FLAT-WIDE | ☐ FLUFFY | ☐ FENCE |

COLOURS AND MARKINGS:

| BIRD'S ACTIONS: | DID THE BIRD SING?:<br>☐ YES  ☐ NO |
|---|---|

## PHOTO/SKETCH

NOTES:

# BIRD WATCHING LOG

| DATE: | TIME: ☐ AM ☐ PM |
|---|---|
| SEASON: | HABITAT: |
| LOCATION: | GPS: |
| WEATHER: | TEMPERATURE: |
| BIRD NAME: | BIRD TYPE: |

| BEAK SHAPE | TAIL | BIRD'S LOCATION |
|---|---|---|
| ☐ CONE | ☐ SHORT | ☐ GROUND |
| ☐ HOOKED | ☐ LONG | ☐ TREE |
| ☐ LONG-THIN | ☐ WIDE | ☐ BUSH |
| ☐ SHORT-POINTED | ☐ THIN | ☐ FEEDER |
| ☐ FLAT-WIDE | ☐ FLUFFY | ☐ FENCE |

COLOURS AND MARKINGS:

| BIRD'S ACTIONS: | DID THE BIRD SING?: ☐ YES ☐ NO |
|---|---|

PHOTO/SKETCH

NOTES:

# BIRD WATCHING LOG

| DATE: | TIME: ☐ AM ☐ PM |
|---|---|
| SEASON: | HABITAT: |
| LOCATION: | GPS: |
| WEATHER: | TEMPERATURE: |
| BIRD NAME: | BIRD TYPE: |

| BEAK SHAPE | TAIL | BIRD'S LOCATION |
|---|---|---|
| ☐ CONE | ☐ SHORT | ☐ GROUND |
| ☐ HOOKED | ☐ LONG | ☐ TREE |
| ☐ LONG-THIN | ☐ WIDE | ☐ BUSH |
| ☐ SHORT-POINTED | ☐ THIN | ☐ FEEDER |
| ☐ FLAT-WIDE | ☐ FLUFFY | ☐ FENCE |

COLOURS AND MARKINGS:

| BIRD'S ACTIONS: | DID THE BIRD SING?: ☐ YES ☐ NO |
|---|---|

## PHOTO/SKETCH

NOTES:

# BIRD WATCHING LOG

| DATE: | TIME: ☐ AM ☐ PM |
|---|---|
| SEASON: | HABITAT: |
| LOCATION: | GPS: |
| WEATHER: | TEMPERATURE: |
| BIRD NAME: | BIRD TYPE: |

| BEAK SHAPE | TAIL | BIRD'S LOCATION |
|---|---|---|
| ☐ CONE | ☐ SHORT | ☐ GROUND |
| ☐ HOOKED | ☐ LONG | ☐ TREE |
| ☐ LONG-THIN | ☐ WIDE | ☐ BUSH |
| ☐ SHORT-POINTED | ☐ THIN | ☐ FEEDER |
| ☐ FLAT-WIDE | ☐ FLUFFY | ☐ FENCE |

COLOURS AND MARKINGS:

| BIRD'S ACTIONS: | DID THE BIRD SING?: ☐ YES ☐ NO |
|---|---|

## PHOTO/SKETCH

NOTES:

# BIRD WATCHING LOG

| DATE: | TIME: ☐ AM ☐ PM |
|---|---|
| SEASON: | HABITAT: |
| LOCATION: | GPS: |
| WEATHER: | TEMPERATURE: |
| BIRD NAME: | BIRD TYPE: |

| BEAK SHAPE | TAIL | BIRD'S LOCATION |
|---|---|---|
| ☐ CONE | ☐ SHORT | ☐ GROUND |
| ☐ HOOKED | ☐ LONG | ☐ TREE |
| ☐ LONG-THIN | ☐ WIDE | ☐ BUSH |
| ☐ SHORT-POINTED | ☐ THIN | ☐ FEEDER |
| ☐ FLAT-WIDE | ☐ FLUFFY | ☐ FENCE |

COLOURS AND MARKINGS:

| BIRD'S ACTIONS: | DID THE BIRD SING?: ☐ YES ☐ NO |
|---|---|

## PHOTO/SKETCH

NOTES:

# BIRD WATCHING LOG

| | |
|---|---|
| DATE: | TIME: ☐ AM ☐ PM |
| SEASON: | HABITAT: |
| LOCATION: | GPS: |
| WEATHER: | TEMPERATURE: |
| BIRD NAME: | BIRD TYPE: |

| BEAK SHAPE | TAIL | BIRD'S LOCATION |
|---|---|---|
| ☐ CONE | ☐ SHORT | ☐ GROUND |
| ☐ HOOKED | ☐ LONG | ☐ TREE |
| ☐ LONG-THIN | ☐ WIDE | ☐ BUSH |
| ☐ SHORT-POINTED | ☐ THIN | ☐ FEEDER |
| ☐ FLAT-WIDE | ☐ FLUFFY | ☐ FENCE |

COLOURS AND MARKINGS:

| BIRD'S ACTIONS: | DID THE BIRD SING?: <br> ☐ YES ☐ NO |
|---|---|

### PHOTO/SKETCH

NOTES:

# BIRD WATCHING LOG

| DATE: | TIME: ☐ AM ☐ PM |
|---|---|
| SEASON: | HABITAT: |
| LOCATION: | GPS: |
| WEATHER: | TEMPERATURE: |
| BIRD NAME: | BIRD TYPE: |

| BEAK SHAPE | TAIL | BIRD'S LOCATION |
|---|---|---|
| ☐ CONE | ☐ SHORT | ☐ GROUND |
| ☐ HOOKED | ☐ LONG | ☐ TREE |
| ☐ LONG-THIN | ☐ WIDE | ☐ BUSH |
| ☐ SHORT-POINTED | ☐ THIN | ☐ FEEDER |
| ☐ FLAT-WIDE | ☐ FLUFFY | ☐ FENCE |

COLOURS AND MARKINGS:

| BIRD'S ACTIONS: | DID THE BIRD SING?:<br>☐ YES   ☐ NO |
|---|---|

PHOTO/SKETCH

NOTES:

# BIRD WATCHING LOG

| DATE: | TIME: ☐ AM ☐ PM |
|---|---|
| SEASON: | HABITAT: |
| LOCATION: | GPS: |
| WEATHER: | TEMPERATURE: |
| BIRD NAME: | BIRD TYPE: |

| BEAK SHAPE | TAIL | BIRD'S LOCATION |
|---|---|---|
| ☐ CONE | ☐ SHORT | ☐ GROUND |
| ☐ HOOKED | ☐ LONG | ☐ TREE |
| ☐ LONG-THIN | ☐ WIDE | ☐ BUSH |
| ☐ SHORT-POINTED | ☐ THIN | ☐ FEEDER |
| ☐ FLAT-WIDE | ☐ FLUFFY | ☐ FENCE |

COLOURS AND MARKINGS:

| BIRD'S ACTIONS: | DID THE BIRD SING?: ☐ YES ☐ NO |
|---|---|

PHOTO/SKETCH

NOTES:

# BIRD WATCHING LOG

| DATE: | TIME: ☐ AM ☐ PM |
|---|---|
| SEASON: | HABITAT: |
| LOCATION: | GPS: |
| WEATHER: | TEMPERATURE: |
| BIRD NAME: | BIRD TYPE: |

| BEAK SHAPE | TAIL | BIRD'S LOCATION |
|---|---|---|
| ☐ CONE | ☐ SHORT | ☐ GROUND |
| ☐ HOOKED | ☐ LONG | ☐ TREE |
| ☐ LONG-THIN | ☐ WIDE | ☐ BUSH |
| ☐ SHORT-POINTED | ☐ THIN | ☐ FEEDER |
| ☐ FLAT-WIDE | ☐ FLUFFY | ☐ FENCE |

COLOURS AND MARKINGS:

| BIRD'S ACTIONS: | DID THE BIRD SING?: ☐ YES ☐ NO |
|---|---|

## PHOTO/SKETCH

NOTES:

# BIRD WATCHING LOG

| DATE: | TIME: ☐ AM ☐ PM |
|---|---|
| SEASON: | HABITAT: |
| LOCATION: | GPS: |
| WEATHER: | TEMPERATURE: |
| BIRD NAME: | BIRD TYPE: |

| BEAK SHAPE | TAIL | BIRD'S LOCATION |
|---|---|---|
| ☐ CONE | ☐ SHORT | ☐ GROUND |
| ☐ HOOKED | ☐ LONG | ☐ TREE |
| ☐ LONG-THIN | ☐ WIDE | ☐ BUSH |
| ☐ SHORT-POINTED | ☐ THIN | ☐ FEEDER |
| ☐ FLAT-WIDE | ☐ FLUFFY | ☐ FENCE |

COLOURS AND MARKINGS:

| BIRD'S ACTIONS: | DID THE BIRD SING?:<br>☐ YES   ☐ NO |
|---|---|

## PHOTO/SKETCH

NOTES:

# BIRD WATCHING LOG

| DATE: | TIME: ☐ AM ☐ PM |
|---|---|
| SEASON: | HABITAT: |
| LOCATION: | GPS: |
| WEATHER: | TEMPERATURE: |
| BIRD NAME: | BIRD TYPE: |

| BEAK SHAPE | TAIL | BIRD'S LOCATION |
|---|---|---|
| ☐ CONE | ☐ SHORT | ☐ GROUND |
| ☐ HOOKED | ☐ LONG | ☐ TREE |
| ☐ LONG-THIN | ☐ WIDE | ☐ BUSH |
| ☐ SHORT-POINTED | ☐ THIN | ☐ FEEDER |
| ☐ FLAT-WIDE | ☐ FLUFFY | ☐ FENCE |

COLOURS AND MARKINGS:

BIRD'S ACTIONS:

DID THE BIRD SING?:
☐ YES ☐ NO

## PHOTO/SKETCH

NOTES:

# BIRD WATCHING LOG

| DATE: | TIME: ☐ AM ☐ PM |
|---|---|
| SEASON: | HABITAT: |
| LOCATION: | GPS: |
| WEATHER: | TEMPERATURE: |
| BIRD NAME: | BIRD TYPE: |

| BEAK SHAPE | TAIL | BIRD'S LOCATION |
|---|---|---|
| ☐ CONE | ☐ SHORT | ☐ GROUND |
| ☐ HOOKED | ☐ LONG | ☐ TREE |
| ☐ LONG-THIN | ☐ WIDE | ☐ BUSH |
| ☐ SHORT-POINTED | ☐ THIN | ☐ FEEDER |
| ☐ FLAT-WIDE | ☐ FLUFFY | ☐ FENCE |

COLOURS AND MARKINGS:

| BIRD'S ACTIONS: | DID THE BIRD SING?: ☐ YES  ☐ NO |
|---|---|

## PHOTO/SKETCH

NOTES:

# BIRD WATCHING LOG

| DATE: | TIME: ☐ AM ☐ PM |
|---|---|
| SEASON: | HABITAT: |
| LOCATION: | GPS: |
| WEATHER: | TEMPERATURE: |
| BIRD NAME: | BIRD TYPE: |

| BEAK SHAPE | TAIL | BIRD'S LOCATION |
|---|---|---|
| ☐ CONE | ☐ SHORT | ☐ GROUND |
| ☐ HOOKED | ☐ LONG | ☐ TREE |
| ☐ LONG-THIN | ☐ WIDE | ☐ BUSH |
| ☐ SHORT-POINTED | ☐ THIN | ☐ FEEDER |
| ☐ FLAT-WIDE | ☐ FLUFFY | ☐ FENCE |

COLOURS AND MARKINGS:

| BIRD'S ACTIONS: | DID THE BIRD SING?: ☐ YES ☐ NO |
|---|---|

## PHOTO/SKETCH

NOTES:

# BIRD WATCHING LOG

| | |
|---|---|
| DATE: | TIME: ☐ AM ☐ PM |
| SEASON: | HABITAT: |
| LOCATION: | GPS: |
| WEATHER: | TEMPERATURE: |
| BIRD NAME: | BIRD TYPE: |

| BEAK SHAPE | TAIL | BIRD'S LOCATION |
|---|---|---|
| ☐ CONE | ☐ SHORT | ☐ GROUND |
| ☐ HOOKED | ☐ LONG | ☐ TREE |
| ☐ LONG-THIN | ☐ WIDE | ☐ BUSH |
| ☐ SHORT-POINTED | ☐ THIN | ☐ FEEDER |
| ☐ FLAT-WIDE | ☐ FLUFFY | ☐ FENCE |

COLOURS AND MARKINGS:

| BIRD'S ACTIONS: | DID THE BIRD SING?: ☐ YES ☐ NO |
|---|---|

## PHOTO/SKETCH

NOTES:

# BIRD WATCHING LOG

| DATE: | TIME: ☐ AM ☐ PM |
|---|---|
| SEASON: | HABITAT: |
| LOCATION: | GPS: |
| WEATHER: | TEMPERATURE: |
| BIRD NAME: | BIRD TYPE: |

| BEAK SHAPE | TAIL | BIRD'S LOCATION |
|---|---|---|
| ☐ CONE | ☐ SHORT | ☐ GROUND |
| ☐ HOOKED | ☐ LONG | ☐ TREE |
| ☐ LONG-THIN | ☐ WIDE | ☐ BUSH |
| ☐ SHORT-POINTED | ☐ THIN | ☐ FEEDER |
| ☐ FLAT-WIDE | ☐ FLUFFY | ☐ FENCE |

COLOURS AND MARKINGS:

| BIRD'S ACTIONS: | DID THE BIRD SING?: ☐ YES  ☐ NO |
|---|---|

## PHOTO/SKETCH

NOTES:

# BIRD WATCHING LOG

| DATE: | TIME: ☐ AM ☐ PM |
|---|---|
| SEASON: | HABITAT: |
| LOCATION: | GPS: |
| WEATHER: | TEMPERATURE: |
| BIRD NAME: | BIRD TYPE: |

| BEAK SHAPE | TAIL | BIRD'S LOCATION |
|---|---|---|
| ☐ CONE | ☐ SHORT | ☐ GROUND |
| ☐ HOOKED | ☐ LONG | ☐ TREE |
| ☐ LONG-THIN | ☐ WIDE | ☐ BUSH |
| ☐ SHORT-POINTED | ☐ THIN | ☐ FEEDER |
| ☐ FLAT-WIDE | ☐ FLUFFY | ☐ FENCE |

COLOURS AND MARKINGS:

| BIRD'S ACTIONS: | DID THE BIRD SING?: ☐ YES ☐ NO |
|---|---|

### PHOTO/SKETCH

NOTES:

# BIRD WATCHING LOG

| | |
|---|---|
| DATE: | TIME: ☐ AM ☐ PM |
| SEASON: | HABITAT: |
| LOCATION: | GPS: |
| WEATHER: | TEMPERATURE: |
| BIRD NAME: | BIRD TYPE: |

| BEAK SHAPE | TAIL | BIRD'S LOCATION |
|---|---|---|
| ☐ CONE | ☐ SHORT | ☐ GROUND |
| ☐ HOOKED | ☐ LONG | ☐ TREE |
| ☐ LONG-THIN | ☐ WIDE | ☐ BUSH |
| ☐ SHORT-POINTED | ☐ THIN | ☐ FEEDER |
| ☐ FLAT-WIDE | ☐ FLUFFY | ☐ FENCE |

COLOURS AND MARKINGS:

| BIRD'S ACTIONS: | DID THE BIRD SING?: |
|---|---|
| | ☐ YES   ☐ NO |

## PHOTO/SKETCH

NOTES:

# BIRD WATCHING LOG

| DATE: | TIME: ☐ AM ☐ PM |
|---|---|
| SEASON: | HABITAT: |
| LOCATION: | GPS: |
| WEATHER: | TEMPERATURE: |
| BIRD NAME: | BIRD TYPE: |

| BEAK SHAPE | TAIL | BIRD'S LOCATION |
|---|---|---|
| ☐ CONE | ☐ SHORT | ☐ GROUND |
| ☐ HOOKED | ☐ LONG | ☐ TREE |
| ☐ LONG-THIN | ☐ WIDE | ☐ BUSH |
| ☐ SHORT-POINTED | ☐ THIN | ☐ FEEDER |
| ☐ FLAT-WIDE | ☐ FLUFFY | ☐ FENCE |

COLOURS AND MARKINGS:

| BIRD'S ACTIONS: | DID THE BIRD SING?: <br> ☐ YES  ☐ NO |
|---|---|

### PHOTO/SKETCH

NOTES:

# BIRD WATCHING LOG

| DATE: | TIME: ☐ AM ☐ PM |
|---|---|
| SEASON: | HABITAT: |
| LOCATION: | GPS: |
| WEATHER: | TEMPERATURE: |
| BIRD NAME: | BIRD TYPE: |

| BEAK SHAPE | TAIL | BIRD'S LOCATION |
|---|---|---|
| ☐ CONE | ☐ SHORT | ☐ GROUND |
| ☐ HOOKED | ☐ LONG | ☐ TREE |
| ☐ LONG-THIN | ☐ WIDE | ☐ BUSH |
| ☐ SHORT-POINTED | ☐ THIN | ☐ FEEDER |
| ☐ FLAT-WIDE | ☐ FLUFFY | ☐ FENCE |

COLOURS AND MARKINGS:

| BIRD'S ACTIONS: | DID THE BIRD SING?: ☐ YES ☐ NO |
|---|---|

PHOTO/SKETCH

NOTES:

# BIRD WATCHING LOG

| DATE: | TIME: ☐ AM ☐ PM |
|---|---|
| SEASON: | HABITAT: |
| LOCATION: | GPS: |
| WEATHER: | TEMPERATURE: |
| BIRD NAME: | BIRD TYPE: |

| BEAK SHAPE | TAIL | BIRD'S LOCATION |
|---|---|---|
| ☐ CONE | ☐ SHORT | ☐ GROUND |
| ☐ HOOKED | ☐ LONG | ☐ TREE |
| ☐ LONG-THIN | ☐ WIDE | ☐ BUSH |
| ☐ SHORT-POINTED | ☐ THIN | ☐ FEEDER |
| ☐ FLAT-WIDE | ☐ FLUFFY | ☐ FENCE |

COLOURS AND MARKINGS:

| BIRD'S ACTIONS: | DID THE BIRD SING?:<br>☐ YES   ☐ NO |
|---|---|

## PHOTO/SKETCH

NOTES:

# BIRD WATCHING LOG

| DATE: | TIME: ☐ AM ☐ PM |
|---|---|
| SEASON: | HABITAT: |
| LOCATION: | GPS: |
| WEATHER: | TEMPERATURE: |
| BIRD NAME: | BIRD TYPE: |

| BEAK SHAPE | TAIL | BIRD'S LOCATION |
|---|---|---|
| ☐ CONE | ☐ SHORT | ☐ GROUND |
| ☐ HOOKED | ☐ LONG | ☐ TREE |
| ☐ LONG-THIN | ☐ WIDE | ☐ BUSH |
| ☐ SHORT-POINTED | ☐ THIN | ☐ FEEDER |
| ☐ FLAT-WIDE | ☐ FLUFFY | ☐ FENCE |

COLOURS AND MARKINGS:

| BIRD'S ACTIONS: | DID THE BIRD SING?: ☐ YES ☐ NO |
|---|---|

## PHOTO/SKETCH

NOTES:

# BIRD WATCHING LOG

| DATE: | TIME: ☐ AM ☐ PM |
|---|---|
| SEASON: | HABITAT: |
| LOCATION: | GPS: |
| WEATHER: | TEMPERATURE: |
| BIRD NAME: | BIRD TYPE: |

| BEAK SHAPE | TAIL | BIRD'S LOCATION |
|---|---|---|
| ☐ CONE | ☐ SHORT | ☐ GROUND |
| ☐ HOOKED | ☐ LONG | ☐ TREE |
| ☐ LONG-THIN | ☐ WIDE | ☐ BUSH |
| ☐ SHORT-POINTED | ☐ THIN | ☐ FEEDER |
| ☐ FLAT-WIDE | ☐ FLUFFY | ☐ FENCE |

COLOURS AND MARKINGS:

| BIRD'S ACTIONS: | DID THE BIRD SING?: ☐ YES ☐ NO |
|---|---|

## PHOTO/SKETCH

NOTES:

# BIRD WATCHING LOG

| DATE: | TIME: ☐ AM ☐ PM |
|---|---|
| SEASON: | HABITAT: |
| LOCATION: | GPS: |
| WEATHER: | TEMPERATURE: |
| BIRD NAME: | BIRD TYPE: |

| BEAK SHAPE | TAIL | BIRD'S LOCATION |
|---|---|---|
| ☐ CONE | ☐ SHORT | ☐ GROUND |
| ☐ HOOKED | ☐ LONG | ☐ TREE |
| ☐ LONG-THIN | ☐ WIDE | ☐ BUSH |
| ☐ SHORT-POINTED | ☐ THIN | ☐ FEEDER |
| ☐ FLAT-WIDE | ☐ FLUFFY | ☐ FENCE |

COLOURS AND MARKINGS:

| BIRD'S ACTIONS: | DID THE BIRD SING?: ☐ YES ☐ NO |
|---|---|

## PHOTO/SKETCH

NOTES:

# BIRD WATCHING LOG

| DATE: | TIME: ☐ AM ☐ PM |
|---|---|
| SEASON: | HABITAT: |
| LOCATION: | GPS: |
| WEATHER: | TEMPERATURE: |
| BIRD NAME: | BIRD TYPE: |

| BEAK SHAPE | TAIL | BIRD'S LOCATION |
|---|---|---|
| ☐ CONE | ☐ SHORT | ☐ GROUND |
| ☐ HOOKED | ☐ LONG | ☐ TREE |
| ☐ LONG-THIN | ☐ WIDE | ☐ BUSH |
| ☐ SHORT-POINTED | ☐ THIN | ☐ FEEDER |
| ☐ FLAT-WIDE | ☐ FLUFFY | ☐ FENCE |

COLOURS AND MARKINGS:

| BIRD'S ACTIONS: | DID THE BIRD SING?:<br>☐ YES ☐ NO |
|---|---|

## PHOTO/SKETCH

NOTES:

# BIRD WATCHING LOG

| DATE: | TIME: ☐ AM ☐ PM |
|---|---|
| SEASON: | HABITAT: |
| LOCATION: | GPS: |
| WEATHER: | TEMPERATURE: |
| BIRD NAME: | BIRD TYPE: |

| BEAK SHAPE | TAIL | BIRD'S LOCATION |
|---|---|---|
| ☐ CONE | ☐ SHORT | ☐ GROUND |
| ☐ HOOKED | ☐ LONG | ☐ TREE |
| ☐ LONG-THIN | ☐ WIDE | ☐ BUSH |
| ☐ SHORT-POINTED | ☐ THIN | ☐ FEEDER |
| ☐ FLAT-WIDE | ☐ FLUFFY | ☐ FENCE |

COLOURS AND MARKINGS:

| BIRD'S ACTIONS: | DID THE BIRD SING?: ☐ YES ☐ NO |
|---|---|

## PHOTO/SKETCH

NOTES:

# BIRD WATCHING LOG

| DATE: | TIME: ☐ AM ☐ PM |
|---|---|
| SEASON: | HABITAT: |
| LOCATION: | GPS: |
| WEATHER: | TEMPERATURE: |
| BIRD NAME: | BIRD TYPE: |

| BEAK SHAPE | TAIL | BIRD'S LOCATION |
|---|---|---|
| ☐ CONE | ☐ SHORT | ☐ GROUND |
| ☐ HOOKED | ☐ LONG | ☐ TREE |
| ☐ LONG-THIN | ☐ WIDE | ☐ BUSH |
| ☐ SHORT-POINTED | ☐ THIN | ☐ FEEDER |
| ☐ FLAT-WIDE | ☐ FLUFFY | ☐ FENCE |

COLOURS AND MARKINGS:

| BIRD'S ACTIONS: | DID THE BIRD SING?: ☐ YES ☐ NO |
|---|---|

### PHOTO/SKETCH

NOTES:

# BIRD WATCHING LOG

| DATE: | TIME: ☐ AM ☐ PM |
|---|---|
| SEASON: | HABITAT: |
| LOCATION: | GPS: |
| WEATHER: | TEMPERATURE: |
| BIRD NAME: | BIRD TYPE: |

| BEAK SHAPE | TAIL | BIRD'S LOCATION |
|---|---|---|
| ☐ CONE | ☐ SHORT | ☐ GROUND |
| ☐ HOOKED | ☐ LONG | ☐ TREE |
| ☐ LONG-THIN | ☐ WIDE | ☐ BUSH |
| ☐ SHORT-POINTED | ☐ THIN | ☐ FEEDER |
| ☐ FLAT-WIDE | ☐ FLUFFY | ☐ FENCE |

COLOURS AND MARKINGS:

| BIRD'S ACTIONS: | DID THE BIRD SING?: <br> ☐ YES   ☐ NO |
|---|---|

## PHOTO/SKETCH

NOTES:

# BIRD WATCHING LOG

| | |
|---|---|
| DATE: | TIME: ☐ AM ☐ PM |
| SEASON: | HABITAT: |
| LOCATION: | GPS: |
| WEATHER: | TEMPERATURE: |
| BIRD NAME: | BIRD TYPE: |

| BEAK SHAPE | TAIL | BIRD'S LOCATION |
|---|---|---|
| ☐ CONE | ☐ SHORT | ☐ GROUND |
| ☐ HOOKED | ☐ LONG | ☐ TREE |
| ☐ LONG-THIN | ☐ WIDE | ☐ BUSH |
| ☐ SHORT-POINTED | ☐ THIN | ☐ FEEDER |
| ☐ FLAT-WIDE | ☐ FLUFFY | ☐ FENCE |

COLOURS AND MARKINGS:

| BIRD'S ACTIONS: | DID THE BIRD SING?:<br>☐ YES  ☐ NO |
|---|---|

## PHOTO/SKETCH

NOTES:

# BIRD WATCHING LOG

| DATE: | TIME: ☐ AM ☐ PM |
|---|---|
| SEASON: | HABITAT: |
| LOCATION: | GPS: |
| WEATHER: | TEMPERATURE: |
| BIRD NAME: | BIRD TYPE: |

| BEAK SHAPE | TAIL | BIRD'S LOCATION |
|---|---|---|
| ☐ CONE | ☐ SHORT | ☐ GROUND |
| ☐ HOOKED | ☐ LONG | ☐ TREE |
| ☐ LONG-THIN | ☐ WIDE | ☐ BUSH |
| ☐ SHORT-POINTED | ☐ THIN | ☐ FEEDER |
| ☐ FLAT-WIDE | ☐ FLUFFY | ☐ FENCE |

COLOURS AND MARKINGS:

BIRD'S ACTIONS: | DID THE BIRD SING?: ☐ YES ☐ NO

## PHOTO/SKETCH

NOTES:

# BIRD WATCHING LOG

| DATE: | TIME: ☐ AM ☐ PM |
|---|---|
| SEASON: | HABITAT: |
| LOCATION: | GPS: |
| WEATHER: | TEMPERATURE: |
| BIRD NAME: | BIRD TYPE: |

| BEAK SHAPE | TAIL | BIRD'S LOCATION |
|---|---|---|
| ☐ CONE | ☐ SHORT | ☐ GROUND |
| ☐ HOOKED | ☐ LONG | ☐ TREE |
| ☐ LONG-THIN | ☐ WIDE | ☐ BUSH |
| ☐ SHORT-POINTED | ☐ THIN | ☐ FEEDER |
| ☐ FLAT-WIDE | ☐ FLUFFY | ☐ FENCE |

COLOURS AND MARKINGS:

| BIRD'S ACTIONS: | DID THE BIRD SING?: ☐ YES ☐ NO |
|---|---|

## PHOTO/SKETCH

NOTES:

# BIRD WATCHING LOG

| DATE: | TIME: ☐ AM ☐ PM |
|---|---|
| SEASON: | HABITAT: |
| LOCATION: | GPS: |
| WEATHER: | TEMPERATURE: |
| BIRD NAME: | BIRD TYPE: |

| BEAK SHAPE | TAIL | BIRD'S LOCATION |
|---|---|---|
| ☐ CONE | ☐ SHORT | ☐ GROUND |
| ☐ HOOKED | ☐ LONG | ☐ TREE |
| ☐ LONG-THIN | ☐ WIDE | ☐ BUSH |
| ☐ SHORT-POINTED | ☐ THIN | ☐ FEEDER |
| ☐ FLAT-WIDE | ☐ FLUFFY | ☐ FENCE |

COLOURS AND MARKINGS:

| BIRD'S ACTIONS: | DID THE BIRD SING?: ☐ YES ☐ NO |
|---|---|

## PHOTO/SKETCH

NOTES:

# BIRD WATCHING LOG

| DATE: | TIME: ☐ AM ☐ PM |
|---|---|
| SEASON: | HABITAT: |
| LOCATION: | GPS: |
| WEATHER: | TEMPERATURE: |
| BIRD NAME: | BIRD TYPE: |

| BEAK SHAPE | TAIL | BIRD'S LOCATION |
|---|---|---|
| ☐ CONE | ☐ SHORT | ☐ GROUND |
| ☐ HOOKED | ☐ LONG | ☐ TREE |
| ☐ LONG-THIN | ☐ WIDE | ☐ BUSH |
| ☐ SHORT-POINTED | ☐ THIN | ☐ FEEDER |
| ☐ FLAT-WIDE | ☐ FLUFFY | ☐ FENCE |

COLOURS AND MARKINGS:

| BIRD'S ACTIONS: | DID THE BIRD SING?: ☐ YES ☐ NO |
|---|---|

## PHOTO/SKETCH

NOTES:

# BIRD WATCHING LOG

| DATE: | TIME: ☐ AM ☐ PM |
|---|---|
| SEASON: | HABITAT: |
| LOCATION: | GPS: |
| WEATHER: | TEMPERATURE: |
| BIRD NAME: | BIRD TYPE: |

| BEAK SHAPE | TAIL | BIRD'S LOCATION |
|---|---|---|
| ☐ CONE | ☐ SHORT | ☐ GROUND |
| ☐ HOOKED | ☐ LONG | ☐ TREE |
| ☐ LONG-THIN | ☐ WIDE | ☐ BUSH |
| ☐ SHORT-POINTED | ☐ THIN | ☐ FEEDER |
| ☐ FLAT-WIDE | ☐ FLUFFY | ☐ FENCE |

COLOURS AND MARKINGS:

| BIRD'S ACTIONS: | DID THE BIRD SING?:<br>☐ YES ☐ NO |
|---|---|

## PHOTO/SKETCH

NOTES:

# BIRD WATCHING LOG

| | |
|---|---|
| DATE: | TIME: ☐ AM ☐ PM |
| SEASON: | HABITAT: |
| LOCATION: | GPS: |
| WEATHER: | TEMPERATURE: |
| BIRD NAME: | BIRD TYPE: |

## BEAK SHAPE

- ☐ CONE
- ☐ HOOKED
- ☐ LONG-THIN
- ☐ SHORT-POINTED
- ☐ FLAT-WIDE

## TAIL

- ☐ SHORT
- ☐ LONG
- ☐ WIDE
- ☐ THIN
- ☐ FLUFFY

## BIRD'S LOCATION

- ☐ GROUND
- ☐ TREE
- ☐ BUSH
- ☐ FEEDER
- ☐ FENCE

COLOURS AND MARKINGS:

BIRD'S ACTIONS:

DID THE BIRD SING?: ☐ YES ☐ NO

## PHOTO/SKETCH

NOTES:

# BIRD WATCHING LOG

| DATE: | TIME: ☐ AM ☐ PM |
|---|---|
| SEASON: | HABITAT: |
| LOCATION: | GPS: |
| WEATHER: | TEMPERATURE: |
| BIRD NAME: | BIRD TYPE: |

| BEAK SHAPE | TAIL | BIRD'S LOCATION |
|---|---|---|
| ☐ CONE | ☐ SHORT | ☐ GROUND |
| ☐ HOOKED | ☐ LONG | ☐ TREE |
| ☐ LONG-THIN | ☐ WIDE | ☐ BUSH |
| ☐ SHORT-POINTED | ☐ THIN | ☐ FEEDER |
| ☐ FLAT-WIDE | ☐ FLUFFY | ☐ FENCE |

COLOURS AND MARKINGS:

| BIRD'S ACTIONS: | DID THE BIRD SING?:<br>☐ YES  ☐ NO |
|---|---|

## PHOTO/SKETCH

NOTES:

# BIRD WATCHING LOG

| | |
|---|---|
| DATE: | TIME: ☐ AM ☐ PM |
| SEASON: | HABITAT: |
| LOCATION: | GPS: |
| WEATHER: | TEMPERATURE: |
| BIRD NAME: | BIRD TYPE: |

| BEAK SHAPE | TAIL | BIRD'S LOCATION |
|---|---|---|
| ☐ CONE | ☐ SHORT | ☐ GROUND |
| ☐ HOOKED | ☐ LONG | ☐ TREE |
| ☐ LONG-THIN | ☐ WIDE | ☐ BUSH |
| ☐ SHORT-POINTED | ☐ THIN | ☐ FEEDER |
| ☐ FLAT-WIDE | ☐ FLUFFY | ☐ FENCE |

COLOURS AND MARKINGS:

| BIRD'S ACTIONS: | DID THE BIRD SING?: ☐ YES ☐ NO |
|---|---|

## PHOTO/SKETCH

NOTES:

# BIRD WATCHING LOG

| DATE: | TIME: ☐ AM ☐ PM |
|---|---|
| SEASON: | HABITAT: |
| LOCATION: | GPS: |
| WEATHER: | TEMPERATURE: |
| BIRD NAME: | BIRD TYPE: |

| BEAK SHAPE | TAIL | BIRD'S LOCATION |
|---|---|---|
| ☐ CONE | ☐ SHORT | ☐ GROUND |
| ☐ HOOKED | ☐ LONG | ☐ TREE |
| ☐ LONG-THIN | ☐ WIDE | ☐ BUSH |
| ☐ SHORT-POINTED | ☐ THIN | ☐ FEEDER |
| ☐ FLAT-WIDE | ☐ FLUFFY | ☐ FENCE |

COLOURS AND MARKINGS:

| BIRD'S ACTIONS: | DID THE BIRD SING?: ☐ YES ☐ NO |
|---|---|

## PHOTO/SKETCH

NOTES:

# BIRD WATCHING LOG

| DATE: | TIME: ☐ AM ☐ PM |
|---|---|
| SEASON: | HABITAT: |
| LOCATION: | GPS: |
| WEATHER: | TEMPERATURE: |
| BIRD NAME: | BIRD TYPE: |

| BEAK SHAPE | TAIL | BIRD'S LOCATION |
|---|---|---|
| ☐ CONE | ☐ SHORT | ☐ GROUND |
| ☐ HOOKED | ☐ LONG | ☐ TREE |
| ☐ LONG-THIN | ☐ WIDE | ☐ BUSH |
| ☐ SHORT-POINTED | ☐ THIN | ☐ FEEDER |
| ☐ FLAT-WIDE | ☐ FLUFFY | ☐ FENCE |

COLOURS AND MARKINGS:

| BIRD'S ACTIONS: | DID THE BIRD SING?: ☐ YES ☐ NO |
|---|---|

## PHOTO/SKETCH

NOTES:

# BIRD WATCHING LOG

| DATE: | TIME: ☐ AM ☐ PM |
|---|---|
| SEASON: | HABITAT: |
| LOCATION: | GPS: |
| WEATHER: | TEMPERATURE: |
| BIRD NAME: | BIRD TYPE: |

| BEAK SHAPE | TAIL | BIRD'S LOCATION |
|---|---|---|
| ☐ CONE | ☐ SHORT | ☐ GROUND |
| ☐ HOOKED | ☐ LONG | ☐ TREE |
| ☐ LONG-THIN | ☐ WIDE | ☐ BUSH |
| ☐ SHORT-POINTED | ☐ THIN | ☐ FEEDER |
| ☐ FLAT-WIDE | ☐ FLUFFY | ☐ FENCE |

COLOURS AND MARKINGS:

| BIRD'S ACTIONS: | DID THE BIRD SING?: ☐ YES  ☐ NO |
|---|---|

## PHOTO/SKETCH

NOTES:

# BIRD WATCHING LOG

| | |
|---|---|
| DATE: | TIME: ☐ AM ☐ PM |
| SEASON: | HABITAT: |
| LOCATION: | GPS: |
| WEATHER: | TEMPERATURE: |
| BIRD NAME: | BIRD TYPE: |

| BEAK SHAPE | TAIL | BIRD'S LOCATION |
|---|---|---|
| ☐ CONE | ☐ SHORT | ☐ GROUND |
| ☐ HOOKED | ☐ LONG | ☐ TREE |
| ☐ LONG-THIN | ☐ WIDE | ☐ BUSH |
| ☐ SHORT-POINTED | ☐ THIN | ☐ FEEDER |
| ☐ FLAT-WIDE | ☐ FLUFFY | ☐ FENCE |

COLOURS AND MARKINGS:

| | |
|---|---|
| BIRD'S ACTIONS: | DID THE BIRD SING?: <br> ☐ YES   ☐ NO |

## PHOTO/SKETCH

NOTES:

# BIRD WATCHING LOG

| DATE: | TIME: ☐ AM ☐ PM |
|---|---|
| SEASON: | HABITAT: |
| LOCATION: | GPS: |
| WEATHER: | TEMPERATURE: |
| BIRD NAME: | BIRD TYPE: |

| BEAK SHAPE | TAIL | BIRD'S LOCATION |
|---|---|---|
| ☐ CONE | ☐ SHORT | ☐ GROUND |
| ☐ HOOKED | ☐ LONG | ☐ TREE |
| ☐ LONG-THIN | ☐ WIDE | ☐ BUSH |
| ☐ SHORT-POINTED | ☐ THIN | ☐ FEEDER |
| ☐ FLAT-WIDE | ☐ FLUFFY | ☐ FENCE |

COLOURS AND MARKINGS:

| BIRD'S ACTIONS: | DID THE BIRD SING?: ☐ YES ☐ NO |
|---|---|

## PHOTO/SKETCH

NOTES:

# BIRD WATCHING LOG

| DATE: | TIME: ☐ AM ☐ PM |
|---|---|
| SEASON: | HABITAT: |
| LOCATION: | GPS: |
| WEATHER: | TEMPERATURE: |
| BIRD NAME: | BIRD TYPE: |

| BEAK SHAPE | TAIL | BIRD'S LOCATION |
|---|---|---|
| ☐ CONE | ☐ SHORT | ☐ GROUND |
| ☐ HOOKED | ☐ LONG | ☐ TREE |
| ☐ LONG-THIN | ☐ WIDE | ☐ BUSH |
| ☐ SHORT-POINTED | ☐ THIN | ☐ FEEDER |
| ☐ FLAT-WIDE | ☐ FLUFFY | ☐ FENCE |

COLOURS AND MARKINGS:

| BIRD'S ACTIONS: | DID THE BIRD SING?: ☐ YES ☐ NO |
|---|---|

## PHOTO/SKETCH

NOTES:

# BIRD WATCHING LOG

| DATE: | TIME: ☐ AM ☐ PM |
|---|---|
| SEASON: | HABITAT: |
| LOCATION: | GPS: |
| WEATHER: | TEMPERATURE: |
| BIRD NAME: | BIRD TYPE: |

| BEAK SHAPE | TAIL | BIRD'S LOCATION |
|---|---|---|
| ☐ CONE | ☐ SHORT | ☐ GROUND |
| ☐ HOOKED | ☐ LONG | ☐ TREE |
| ☐ LONG-THIN | ☐ WIDE | ☐ BUSH |
| ☐ SHORT-POINTED | ☐ THIN | ☐ FEEDER |
| ☐ FLAT-WIDE | ☐ FLUFFY | ☐ FENCE |

COLOURS AND MARKINGS:

| BIRD'S ACTIONS: | DID THE BIRD SING?: ☐ YES ☐ NO |
|---|---|

## PHOTO/SKETCH

NOTES:

# BIRD WATCHING LOG

| DATE: | TIME: ☐ AM ☐ PM |
|---|---|
| SEASON: | HABITAT: |
| LOCATION: | GPS: |
| WEATHER: | TEMPERATURE: |
| BIRD NAME: | BIRD TYPE: |

| BEAK SHAPE | TAIL | BIRD'S LOCATION |
|---|---|---|
| ☐ CONE | ☐ SHORT | ☐ GROUND |
| ☐ HOOKED | ☐ LONG | ☐ TREE |
| ☐ LONG-THIN | ☐ WIDE | ☐ BUSH |
| ☐ SHORT-POINTED | ☐ THIN | ☐ FEEDER |
| ☐ FLAT-WIDE | ☐ FLUFFY | ☐ FENCE |

COLOURS AND MARKINGS:

| BIRD'S ACTIONS: | DID THE BIRD SING?: ☐ YES ☐ NO |
|---|---|

## PHOTO/SKETCH

NOTES:

# BIRD WATCHING LOG

| DATE: | TIME: ☐ AM ☐ PM |
|---|---|
| SEASON: | HABITAT: |
| LOCATION: | GPS: |
| WEATHER: | TEMPERATURE: |
| BIRD NAME: | BIRD TYPE: |

| BEAK SHAPE | TAIL | BIRD'S LOCATION |
|---|---|---|
| ☐ CONE | ☐ SHORT | ☐ GROUND |
| ☐ HOOKED | ☐ LONG | ☐ TREE |
| ☐ LONG-THIN | ☐ WIDE | ☐ BUSH |
| ☐ SHORT-POINTED | ☐ THIN | ☐ FEEDER |
| ☐ FLAT-WIDE | ☐ FLUFFY | ☐ FENCE |

COLOURS AND MARKINGS:

| BIRD'S ACTIONS: | DID THE BIRD SING?: ☐ YES ☐ NO |
|---|---|

## PHOTO/SKETCH

NOTES:

# BIRD WATCHING LOG

| DATE: | TIME: ☐ AM ☐ PM |
|---|---|
| SEASON: | HABITAT: |
| LOCATION: | GPS: |
| WEATHER: | TEMPERATURE: |
| BIRD NAME: | BIRD TYPE: |

| BEAK SHAPE | TAIL | BIRD'S LOCATION |
|---|---|---|
| ☐ CONE | ☐ SHORT | ☐ GROUND |
| ☐ HOOKED | ☐ LONG | ☐ TREE |
| ☐ LONG-THIN | ☐ WIDE | ☐ BUSH |
| ☐ SHORT-POINTED | ☐ THIN | ☐ FEEDER |
| ☐ FLAT-WIDE | ☐ FLUFFY | ☐ FENCE |

COLOURS AND MARKINGS:

| BIRD'S ACTIONS: | DID THE BIRD SING?: ☐ YES ☐ NO |
|---|---|

## PHOTO/SKETCH

NOTES:

# BIRD WATCHING LOG

| | |
|---|---|
| DATE: | TIME: ☐ AM ☐ PM |
| SEASON: | HABITAT: |
| LOCATION: | GPS: |
| WEATHER: | TEMPERATURE: |
| BIRD NAME: | BIRD TYPE: |

| BEAK SHAPE | TAIL | BIRD'S LOCATION |
|---|---|---|
| ☐ CONE | ☐ SHORT | ☐ GROUND |
| ☐ HOOKED | ☐ LONG | ☐ TREE |
| ☐ LONG-THIN | ☐ WIDE | ☐ BUSH |
| ☐ SHORT-POINTED | ☐ THIN | ☐ FEEDER |
| ☐ FLAT-WIDE | ☐ FLUFFY | ☐ FENCE |

COLOURS AND MARKINGS:

| | |
|---|---|
| BIRD'S ACTIONS: | DID THE BIRD SING?: ☐ YES  ☐ NO |

## PHOTO/SKETCH

NOTES:

# BIRD WATCHING LOG

| DATE: | TIME: ☐ AM ☐ PM |
|---|---|
| SEASON: | HABITAT: |
| LOCATION: | GPS: |
| WEATHER: | TEMPERATURE: |
| BIRD NAME: | BIRD TYPE: |

| BEAK SHAPE | TAIL | BIRD'S LOCATION |
|---|---|---|
| ☐ CONE | ☐ SHORT | ☐ GROUND |
| ☐ HOOKED | ☐ LONG | ☐ TREE |
| ☐ LONG-THIN | ☐ WIDE | ☐ BUSH |
| ☐ SHORT-POINTED | ☐ THIN | ☐ FEEDER |
| ☐ FLAT-WIDE | ☐ FLUFFY | ☐ FENCE |

COLOURS AND MARKINGS:

| BIRD'S ACTIONS: | DID THE BIRD SING?: ☐ YES ☐ NO |
|---|---|

## PHOTO/SKETCH

NOTES:

# BIRD WATCHING LOG

| DATE: | TIME: ☐ AM ☐ PM |
|---|---|
| SEASON: | HABITAT: |
| LOCATION: | GPS: |
| WEATHER: | TEMPERATURE: |
| BIRD NAME: | BIRD TYPE: |

| BEAK SHAPE | TAIL | BIRD'S LOCATION |
|---|---|---|
| ☐ CONE | ☐ SHORT | ☐ GROUND |
| ☐ HOOKED | ☐ LONG | ☐ TREE |
| ☐ LONG-THIN | ☐ WIDE | ☐ BUSH |
| ☐ SHORT-POINTED | ☐ THIN | ☐ FEEDER |
| ☐ FLAT-WIDE | ☐ FLUFFY | ☐ FENCE |

COLOURS AND MARKINGS:

| BIRD'S ACTIONS: | DID THE BIRD SING?: ☐ YES ☐ NO |
|---|---|

## PHOTO/SKETCH

NOTES:

# BIRD WATCHING LOG

| DATE: | TIME: ☐ AM ☐ PM |
|---|---|
| SEASON: | HABITAT: |
| LOCATION: | GPS: |
| WEATHER: | TEMPERATURE: |
| BIRD NAME: | BIRD TYPE: |

| BEAK SHAPE | TAIL | BIRD'S LOCATION |
|---|---|---|
| ☐ CONE | ☐ SHORT | ☐ GROUND |
| ☐ HOOKED | ☐ LONG | ☐ TREE |
| ☐ LONG-THIN | ☐ WIDE | ☐ BUSH |
| ☐ SHORT-POINTED | ☐ THIN | ☐ FEEDER |
| ☐ FLAT-WIDE | ☐ FLUFFY | ☐ FENCE |

COLOURS AND MARKINGS:

| BIRD'S ACTIONS: | DID THE BIRD SING?: <br> ☐ YES ☐ NO |
|---|---|

## PHOTO/SKETCH

NOTES:

# BIRD WATCHING LOG

| DATE: | TIME: ☐ AM ☐ PM |
|---|---|
| SEASON: | HABITAT: |
| LOCATION: | GPS: |
| WEATHER: | TEMPERATURE: |
| BIRD NAME: | BIRD TYPE: |

| BEAK SHAPE | TAIL | BIRD'S LOCATION |
|---|---|---|
| ☐ CONE | ☐ SHORT | ☐ GROUND |
| ☐ HOOKED | ☐ LONG | ☐ TREE |
| ☐ LONG-THIN | ☐ WIDE | ☐ BUSH |
| ☐ SHORT-POINTED | ☐ THIN | ☐ FEEDER |
| ☐ FLAT-WIDE | ☐ FLUFFY | ☐ FENCE |

COLOURS AND MARKINGS:

| BIRD'S ACTIONS: | DID THE BIRD SING?: <br> ☐ YES   ☐ NO |
|---|---|

## PHOTO/SKETCH

NOTES:

# BIRD WATCHING LOG

| | |
|---|---|
| DATE: | TIME: ☐ AM ☐ PM |
| SEASON: | HABITAT: |
| LOCATION: | GPS: |
| WEATHER: | TEMPERATURE: |
| BIRD NAME: | BIRD TYPE: |

| BEAK SHAPE | TAIL | BIRD'S LOCATION |
|---|---|---|
| ☐ CONE | ☐ SHORT | ☐ GROUND |
| ☐ HOOKED | ☐ LONG | ☐ TREE |
| ☐ LONG-THIN | ☐ WIDE | ☐ BUSH |
| ☐ SHORT-POINTED | ☐ THIN | ☐ FEEDER |
| ☐ FLAT-WIDE | ☐ FLUFFY | ☐ FENCE |

COLOURS AND MARKINGS:

| BIRD'S ACTIONS: | DID THE BIRD SING?: ☐ YES    ☐ NO |
|---|---|

### PHOTO/SKETCH

NOTES:

# BIRD WATCHING LOG

| | |
|---|---|
| DATE: | TIME: ☐ AM ☐ PM |
| SEASON: | HABITAT: |
| LOCATION: | GPS: |
| WEATHER: | TEMPERATURE: |
| BIRD NAME: | BIRD TYPE: |

| BEAK SHAPE | TAIL | BIRD'S LOCATION |
|---|---|---|
| ☐ CONE | ☐ SHORT | ☐ GROUND |
| ☐ HOOKED | ☐ LONG | ☐ TREE |
| ☐ LONG-THIN | ☐ WIDE | ☐ BUSH |
| ☐ SHORT-POINTED | ☐ THIN | ☐ FEEDER |
| ☐ FLAT-WIDE | ☐ FLUFFY | ☐ FENCE |

COLOURS AND MARKINGS:

| | |
|---|---|
| BIRD'S ACTIONS: | DID THE BIRD SING?: ☐ YES ☐ NO |

## PHOTO/SKETCH

NOTES:

# BIRD WATCHING LOG

| DATE: | TIME: ☐ AM ☐ PM |
|---|---|
| SEASON: | HABITAT: |
| LOCATION: | GPS: |
| WEATHER: | TEMPERATURE: |
| BIRD NAME: | BIRD TYPE: |

| BEAK SHAPE | TAIL | BIRD'S LOCATION |
|---|---|---|
| ☐ CONE | ☐ SHORT | ☐ GROUND |
| ☐ HOOKED | ☐ LONG | ☐ TREE |
| ☐ LONG-THIN | ☐ WIDE | ☐ BUSH |
| ☐ SHORT-POINTED | ☐ THIN | ☐ FEEDER |
| ☐ FLAT-WIDE | ☐ FLUFFY | ☐ FENCE |

COLOURS AND MARKINGS:

| BIRD'S ACTIONS: | DID THE BIRD SING?: ☐ YES ☐ NO |
|---|---|

### PHOTO/SKETCH

NOTES:

# BIRD WATCHING LOG

| | |
|---|---|
| DATE: | TIME: ☐ AM ☐ PM |
| SEASON: | HABITAT: |
| LOCATION: | GPS: |
| WEATHER: | TEMPERATURE: |
| BIRD NAME: | BIRD TYPE: |

| BEAK SHAPE | TAIL | BIRD'S LOCATION |
|---|---|---|
| ☐ CONE | ☐ SHORT | ☐ GROUND |
| ☐ HOOKED | ☐ LONG | ☐ TREE |
| ☐ LONG-THIN | ☐ WIDE | ☐ BUSH |
| ☐ SHORT-POINTED | ☐ THIN | ☐ FEEDER |
| ☐ FLAT-WIDE | ☐ FLUFFY | ☐ FENCE |

COLOURS AND MARKINGS:

| | |
|---|---|
| BIRD'S ACTIONS: | DID THE BIRD SING?: <br> ☐ YES   ☐ NO |

## PHOTO/SKETCH

NOTES:

# BIRD WATCHING LOG

| DATE: | TIME: ☐ AM ☐ PM |
|---|---|
| SEASON: | HABITAT: |
| LOCATION: | GPS: |
| WEATHER: | TEMPERATURE: |
| BIRD NAME: | BIRD TYPE: |

| BEAK SHAPE | TAIL | BIRD'S LOCATION |
|---|---|---|
| ☐ CONE | ☐ SHORT | ☐ GROUND |
| ☐ HOOKED | ☐ LONG | ☐ TREE |
| ☐ LONG-THIN | ☐ WIDE | ☐ BUSH |
| ☐ SHORT-POINTED | ☐ THIN | ☐ FEEDER |
| ☐ FLAT-WIDE | ☐ FLUFFY | ☐ FENCE |

COLOURS AND MARKINGS:

| BIRD'S ACTIONS: | DID THE BIRD SING?: ☐ YES ☐ NO |
|---|---|

## PHOTO/SKETCH

NOTES:

# BIRD WATCHING LOG

| DATE: | TIME: ☐ AM ☐ PM |
|---|---|
| SEASON: | HABITAT: |
| LOCATION: | GPS: |
| WEATHER: | TEMPERATURE: |
| BIRD NAME: | BIRD TYPE: |

| BEAK SHAPE | TAIL | BIRD'S LOCATION |
|---|---|---|
| ☐ CONE | ☐ SHORT | ☐ GROUND |
| ☐ HOOKED | ☐ LONG | ☐ TREE |
| ☐ LONG-THIN | ☐ WIDE | ☐ BUSH |
| ☐ SHORT-POINTED | ☐ THIN | ☐ FEEDER |
| ☐ FLAT-WIDE | ☐ FLUFFY | ☐ FENCE |

COLOURS AND MARKINGS:

| BIRD'S ACTIONS: | DID THE BIRD SING?:<br>☐ YES   ☐ NO |
|---|---|

## PHOTO/SKETCH

NOTES:

# BIRD WATCHING LOG

| DATE: | TIME: ☐ AM ☐ PM |
|---|---|
| SEASON: | HABITAT: |
| LOCATION: | GPS: |
| WEATHER: | TEMPERATURE: |
| BIRD NAME: | BIRD TYPE: |

| BEAK SHAPE | TAIL | BIRD'S LOCATION |
|---|---|---|
| ☐ CONE | ☐ SHORT | ☐ GROUND |
| ☐ HOOKED | ☐ LONG | ☐ TREE |
| ☐ LONG-THIN | ☐ WIDE | ☐ BUSH |
| ☐ SHORT-POINTED | ☐ THIN | ☐ FEEDER |
| ☐ FLAT-WIDE | ☐ FLUFFY | ☐ FENCE |

COLOURS AND MARKINGS:

| BIRD'S ACTIONS: | DID THE BIRD SING?: ☐ YES ☐ NO |
|---|---|

## PHOTO/SKETCH

NOTES:

# BIRD WATCHING LOG

| DATE: | TIME: ☐ AM ☐ PM |
|---|---|
| SEASON: | HABITAT: |
| LOCATION: | GPS: |
| WEATHER: | TEMPERATURE: |
| BIRD NAME: | BIRD TYPE: |

| BEAK SHAPE | TAIL | BIRD'S LOCATION |
|---|---|---|
| ☐ CONE | ☐ SHORT | ☐ GROUND |
| ☐ HOOKED | ☐ LONG | ☐ TREE |
| ☐ LONG-THIN | ☐ WIDE | ☐ BUSH |
| ☐ SHORT-POINTED | ☐ THIN | ☐ FEEDER |
| ☐ FLAT-WIDE | ☐ FLUFFY | ☐ FENCE |

COLOURS AND MARKINGS:

| BIRD'S ACTIONS: | DID THE BIRD SING?: ☐ YES  ☐ NO |
|---|---|

## PHOTO/SKETCH

NOTES:

# BIRD WATCHING LOG

| DATE: | TIME: ☐ AM ☐ PM |
|---|---|
| SEASON: | HABITAT: |
| LOCATION: | GPS: |
| WEATHER: | TEMPERATURE: |
| BIRD NAME: | BIRD TYPE: |

| BEAK SHAPE | TAIL | BIRD'S LOCATION |
|---|---|---|
| ☐ CONE | ☐ SHORT | ☐ GROUND |
| ☐ HOOKED | ☐ LONG | ☐ TREE |
| ☐ LONG-THIN | ☐ WIDE | ☐ BUSH |
| ☐ SHORT-POINTED | ☐ THIN | ☐ FEEDER |
| ☐ FLAT-WIDE | ☐ FLUFFY | ☐ FENCE |

COLOURS AND MARKINGS:

| BIRD'S ACTIONS: | DID THE BIRD SING?: ☐ YES   ☐ NO |
|---|---|

## PHOTO/SKETCH

NOTES:

# BIRD WATCHING LOG

| DATE: | TIME: ☐ AM ☐ PM |
|---|---|
| SEASON: | HABITAT: |
| LOCATION: | GPS: |
| WEATHER: | TEMPERATURE: |
| BIRD NAME: | BIRD TYPE: |

| BEAK SHAPE | TAIL | BIRD'S LOCATION |
|---|---|---|
| ☐ CONE | ☐ SHORT | ☐ GROUND |
| ☐ HOOKED | ☐ LONG | ☐ TREE |
| ☐ LONG-THIN | ☐ WIDE | ☐ BUSH |
| ☐ SHORT-POINTED | ☐ THIN | ☐ FEEDER |
| ☐ FLAT-WIDE | ☐ FLUFFY | ☐ FENCE |

COLOURS AND MARKINGS:

| BIRD'S ACTIONS: | DID THE BIRD SING?: ☐ YES ☐ NO |
|---|---|

## PHOTO/SKETCH

NOTES:

# BIRD WATCHING LOG

| | |
|---|---|
| DATE: | TIME: ☐ AM ☐ PM |
| SEASON: | HABITAT: |
| LOCATION: | GPS: |
| WEATHER: | TEMPERATURE: |
| BIRD NAME: | BIRD TYPE: |

| BEAK SHAPE | TAIL | BIRD'S LOCATION |
|---|---|---|
| ☐ CONE | ☐ SHORT | ☐ GROUND |
| ☐ HOOKED | ☐ LONG | ☐ TREE |
| ☐ LONG-THIN | ☐ WIDE | ☐ BUSH |
| ☐ SHORT-POINTED | ☐ THIN | ☐ FEEDER |
| ☐ FLAT-WIDE | ☐ FLUFFY | ☐ FENCE |

COLOURS AND MARKINGS:

| BIRD'S ACTIONS: | DID THE BIRD SING?: |
|---|---|
| | ☐ YES ☐ NO |

## PHOTO/SKETCH

NOTES:

# BIRD WATCHING LOG

| DATE: | TIME: ☐ AM ☐ PM |
|---|---|
| SEASON: | HABITAT: |
| LOCATION: | GPS: |
| WEATHER: | TEMPERATURE: |
| BIRD NAME: | BIRD TYPE: |

| BEAK SHAPE | TAIL | BIRD'S LOCATION |
|---|---|---|
| ☐ CONE | ☐ SHORT | ☐ GROUND |
| ☐ HOOKED | ☐ LONG | ☐ TREE |
| ☐ LONG-THIN | ☐ WIDE | ☐ BUSH |
| ☐ SHORT-POINTED | ☐ THIN | ☐ FEEDER |
| ☐ FLAT-WIDE | ☐ FLUFFY | ☐ FENCE |

COLOURS AND MARKINGS:

| BIRD'S ACTIONS: | DID THE BIRD SING?:<br>☐ YES   ☐ NO |
|---|---|

## PHOTO/SKETCH

NOTES:

# BIRD WATCHING LOG

| DATE: | TIME: ☐ AM ☐ PM |
|---|---|
| SEASON: | HABITAT: |
| LOCATION: | GPS: |
| WEATHER: | TEMPERATURE: |
| BIRD NAME: | BIRD TYPE: |

| BEAK SHAPE | TAIL | BIRD'S LOCATION |
|---|---|---|
| ☐ CONE | ☐ SHORT | ☐ GROUND |
| ☐ HOOKED | ☐ LONG | ☐ TREE |
| ☐ LONG-THIN | ☐ WIDE | ☐ BUSH |
| ☐ SHORT-POINTED | ☐ THIN | ☐ FEEDER |
| ☐ FLAT-WIDE | ☐ FLUFFY | ☐ FENCE |

COLOURS AND MARKINGS:

| BIRD'S ACTIONS: | DID THE BIRD SING?: ☐ YES ☐ NO |
|---|---|

### PHOTO/SKETCH

NOTES:

# BIRD WATCHING LOG

| DATE: | TIME: ☐ AM ☐ PM |
|---|---|
| SEASON: | HABITAT: |
| LOCATION: | GPS: |
| WEATHER: | TEMPERATURE: |
| BIRD NAME: | BIRD TYPE: |

| BEAK SHAPE | TAIL | BIRD'S LOCATION |
|---|---|---|
| ☐ CONE | ☐ SHORT | ☐ GROUND |
| ☐ HOOKED | ☐ LONG | ☐ TREE |
| ☐ LONG-THIN | ☐ WIDE | ☐ BUSH |
| ☐ SHORT-POINTED | ☐ THIN | ☐ FEEDER |
| ☐ FLAT-WIDE | ☐ FLUFFY | ☐ FENCE |

COLOURS AND MARKINGS:

| BIRD'S ACTIONS: | DID THE BIRD SING?: ☐ YES  ☐ NO |
|---|---|

### PHOTO/SKETCH

NOTES:

# BIRD WATCHING LOG

| | |
|---|---|
| DATE: | TIME: ☐ AM ☐ PM |
| SEASON: | HABITAT: |
| LOCATION: | GPS: |
| WEATHER: | TEMPERATURE: |
| BIRD NAME: | BIRD TYPE: |

| BEAK SHAPE | TAIL | BIRD'S LOCATION |
|---|---|---|
| ☐ CONE | ☐ SHORT | ☐ GROUND |
| ☐ HOOKED | ☐ LONG | ☐ TREE |
| ☐ LONG-THIN | ☐ WIDE | ☐ BUSH |
| ☐ SHORT-POINTED | ☐ THIN | ☐ FEEDER |
| ☐ FLAT-WIDE | ☐ FLUFFY | ☐ FENCE |

COLOURS AND MARKINGS:

| BIRD'S ACTIONS: | DID THE BIRD SING?: <br> ☐ YES ☐ NO |
|---|---|

## PHOTO/SKETCH

NOTES:

# BIRD WATCHING LOG

| DATE: | TIME: ☐ AM ☐ PM |
|---|---|
| SEASON: | HABITAT: |
| LOCATION: | GPS: |
| WEATHER: | TEMPERATURE: |
| BIRD NAME: | BIRD TYPE: |

| BEAK SHAPE | TAIL | BIRD'S LOCATION |
|---|---|---|
| ☐ CONE | ☐ SHORT | ☐ GROUND |
| ☐ HOOKED | ☐ LONG | ☐ TREE |
| ☐ LONG-THIN | ☐ WIDE | ☐ BUSH |
| ☐ SHORT-POINTED | ☐ THIN | ☐ FEEDER |
| ☐ FLAT-WIDE | ☐ FLUFFY | ☐ FENCE |

COLOURS AND MARKINGS:

| BIRD'S ACTIONS: | DID THE BIRD SING?:<br>☐ YES   ☐ NO |
|---|---|

### PHOTO/SKETCH

NOTES:

# BIRD WATCHING LOG

| DATE: | TIME: ☐ AM ☐ PM |
|---|---|
| SEASON: | HABITAT: |
| LOCATION: | GPS: |
| WEATHER: | TEMPERATURE: |
| BIRD NAME: | BIRD TYPE: |

| BEAK SHAPE | TAIL | BIRD'S LOCATION |
|---|---|---|
| ☐ CONE | ☐ SHORT | ☐ GROUND |
| ☐ HOOKED | ☐ LONG | ☐ TREE |
| ☐ LONG-THIN | ☐ WIDE | ☐ BUSH |
| ☐ SHORT-POINTED | ☐ THIN | ☐ FEEDER |
| ☐ FLAT-WIDE | ☐ FLUFFY | ☐ FENCE |

COLOURS AND MARKINGS:

| BIRD'S ACTIONS: | DID THE BIRD SING?: ☐ YES  ☐ NO |
|---|---|

## PHOTO/SKETCH

NOTES:

# BIRD WATCHING LOG

| DATE: | TIME: ☐ AM ☐ PM |
|---|---|
| SEASON: | HABITAT: |
| LOCATION: | GPS: |
| WEATHER: | TEMPERATURE: |
| BIRD NAME: | BIRD TYPE: |

| BEAK SHAPE | TAIL | BIRD'S LOCATION |
|---|---|---|
| ☐ CONE | ☐ SHORT | ☐ GROUND |
| ☐ HOOKED | ☐ LONG | ☐ TREE |
| ☐ LONG-THIN | ☐ WIDE | ☐ BUSH |
| ☐ SHORT-POINTED | ☐ THIN | ☐ FEEDER |
| ☐ FLAT-WIDE | ☐ FLUFFY | ☐ FENCE |

COLOURS AND MARKINGS:

| BIRD'S ACTIONS: | DID THE BIRD SING?: ☐ YES ☐ NO |
|---|---|

## PHOTO/SKETCH

NOTES:

# BIRD WATCHING LOG

| DATE: | TIME: ☐ AM ☐ PM |
|---|---|
| SEASON: | HABITAT: |
| LOCATION: | GPS: |
| WEATHER: | TEMPERATURE: |
| BIRD NAME: | BIRD TYPE: |

| BEAK SHAPE | TAIL | BIRD'S LOCATION |
|---|---|---|
| ☐ CONE | ☐ SHORT | ☐ GROUND |
| ☐ HOOKED | ☐ LONG | ☐ TREE |
| ☐ LONG-THIN | ☐ WIDE | ☐ BUSH |
| ☐ SHORT-POINTED | ☐ THIN | ☐ FEEDER |
| ☐ FLAT-WIDE | ☐ FLUFFY | ☐ FENCE |

COLOURS AND MARKINGS:

| BIRD'S ACTIONS: | DID THE BIRD SING?: ☐ YES ☐ NO |
|---|---|

## PHOTO/SKETCH

NOTES:

# BIRD WATCHING LOG

| DATE: | TIME: ☐ AM ☐ PM |
|---|---|
| SEASON: | HABITAT: |
| LOCATION: | GPS: |
| WEATHER: | TEMPERATURE: |
| BIRD NAME: | BIRD TYPE: |

| BEAK SHAPE | TAIL | BIRD'S LOCATION |
|---|---|---|
| ☐ CONE | ☐ SHORT | ☐ GROUND |
| ☐ HOOKED | ☐ LONG | ☐ TREE |
| ☐ LONG-THIN | ☐ WIDE | ☐ BUSH |
| ☐ SHORT-POINTED | ☐ THIN | ☐ FEEDER |
| ☐ FLAT-WIDE | ☐ FLUFFY | ☐ FENCE |

COLOURS AND MARKINGS:

| BIRD'S ACTIONS: | DID THE BIRD SING?: ☐ YES ☐ NO |
|---|---|

## PHOTO/SKETCH

NOTES:

# BIRD WATCHING LOG

| | |
|---|---|
| DATE: | TIME: ☐ AM ☐ PM |
| SEASON: | HABITAT: |
| LOCATION: | GPS: |
| WEATHER: | TEMPERATURE: |
| BIRD NAME: | BIRD TYPE: |

| BEAK SHAPE | TAIL | BIRD'S LOCATION |
|---|---|---|
| ☐ CONE | ☐ SHORT | ☐ GROUND |
| ☐ HOOKED | ☐ LONG | ☐ TREE |
| ☐ LONG-THIN | ☐ WIDE | ☐ BUSH |
| ☐ SHORT-POINTED | ☐ THIN | ☐ FEEDER |
| ☐ FLAT-WIDE | ☐ FLUFFY | ☐ FENCE |

COLOURS AND MARKINGS:

| BIRD'S ACTIONS: | DID THE BIRD SING?: ☐ YES  ☐ NO |
|---|---|

## PHOTO/SKETCH

NOTES:

# BIRD WATCHING LOG

| DATE: | TIME: ☐ AM ☐ PM |
|---|---|
| SEASON: | HABITAT: |
| LOCATION: | GPS: |
| WEATHER: | TEMPERATURE: |
| BIRD NAME: | BIRD TYPE: |

| BEAK SHAPE | TAIL | BIRD'S LOCATION |
|---|---|---|
| ☐ CONE | ☐ SHORT | ☐ GROUND |
| ☐ HOOKED | ☐ LONG | ☐ TREE |
| ☐ LONG-THIN | ☐ WIDE | ☐ BUSH |
| ☐ SHORT-POINTED | ☐ THIN | ☐ FEEDER |
| ☐ FLAT-WIDE | ☐ FLUFFY | ☐ FENCE |

COLOURS AND MARKINGS:

| BIRD'S ACTIONS: | DID THE BIRD SING?: ☐ YES  ☐ NO |
|---|---|

## PHOTO/SKETCH

NOTES:

# BIRD WATCHING LOG

| DATE: | TIME: ☐ AM ☐ PM |
|---|---|
| SEASON: | HABITAT: |
| LOCATION: | GPS: |
| WEATHER: | TEMPERATURE: |
| BIRD NAME: | BIRD TYPE: |

| BEAK SHAPE | TAIL | BIRD'S LOCATION |
|---|---|---|
| ☐ CONE | ☐ SHORT | ☐ GROUND |
| ☐ HOOKED | ☐ LONG | ☐ TREE |
| ☐ LONG-THIN | ☐ WIDE | ☐ BUSH |
| ☐ SHORT-POINTED | ☐ THIN | ☐ FEEDER |
| ☐ FLAT-WIDE | ☐ FLUFFY | ☐ FENCE |

COLOURS AND MARKINGS:

| BIRD'S ACTIONS: | DID THE BIRD SING?: ☐ YES ☐ NO |
|---|---|

### PHOTO/SKETCH

NOTES:

# BIRD WATCHING LOG

| DATE: | TIME: ☐ AM ☐ PM |
|---|---|
| SEASON: | HABITAT: |
| LOCATION: | GPS: |
| WEATHER: | TEMPERATURE: |
| BIRD NAME: | BIRD TYPE: |

| BEAK SHAPE | TAIL | BIRD'S LOCATION |
|---|---|---|
| ☐ CONE | ☐ SHORT | ☐ GROUND |
| ☐ HOOKED | ☐ LONG | ☐ TREE |
| ☐ LONG-THIN | ☐ WIDE | ☐ BUSH |
| ☐ SHORT-POINTED | ☐ THIN | ☐ FEEDER |
| ☐ FLAT-WIDE | ☐ FLUFFY | ☐ FENCE |

COLOURS AND MARKINGS:

BIRD'S ACTIONS:                     DID THE BIRD SING?:
                                    ☐ YES    ☐ NO

PHOTO/SKETCH

NOTES:

# BIRD WATCHING LOG

| DATE: | TIME: ☐ AM ☐ PM |
|---|---|
| SEASON: | HABITAT: |
| LOCATION: | GPS: |
| WEATHER: | TEMPERATURE: |
| BIRD NAME: | BIRD TYPE: |

| BEAK SHAPE | TAIL | BIRD'S LOCATION |
|---|---|---|
| ☐ CONE | ☐ SHORT | ☐ GROUND |
| ☐ HOOKED | ☐ LONG | ☐ TREE |
| ☐ LONG-THIN | ☐ WIDE | ☐ BUSH |
| ☐ SHORT-POINTED | ☐ THIN | ☐ FEEDER |
| ☐ FLAT-WIDE | ☐ FLUFFY | ☐ FENCE |

COLOURS AND MARKINGS:

| BIRD'S ACTIONS: | DID THE BIRD SING?:<br>☐ YES ☐ NO |
|---|---|

## PHOTO/SKETCH

NOTES:

# BIRD WATCHING LOG

| DATE: | TIME: ☐ AM ☐ PM |
|---|---|
| SEASON: | HABITAT: |
| LOCATION: | GPS: |
| WEATHER: | TEMPERATURE: |
| BIRD NAME: | BIRD TYPE: |

| BEAK SHAPE | TAIL | BIRD'S LOCATION |
|---|---|---|
| ☐ CONE | ☐ SHORT | ☐ GROUND |
| ☐ HOOKED | ☐ LONG | ☐ TREE |
| ☐ LONG-THIN | ☐ WIDE | ☐ BUSH |
| ☐ SHORT-POINTED | ☐ THIN | ☐ FEEDER |
| ☐ FLAT-WIDE | ☐ FLUFFY | ☐ FENCE |

COLOURS AND MARKINGS:

| BIRD'S ACTIONS: | DID THE BIRD SING?: ☐ YES   ☐ NO |
|---|---|

### PHOTO/SKETCH

NOTES:

# BIRD WATCHING LOG

| DATE: | TIME: ☐ AM ☐ PM |
|---|---|
| SEASON: | HABITAT: |
| LOCATION: | GPS: |
| WEATHER: | TEMPERATURE: |
| BIRD NAME: | BIRD TYPE: |

| BEAK SHAPE | TAIL | BIRD'S LOCATION |
|---|---|---|
| ☐ CONE | ☐ SHORT | ☐ GROUND |
| ☐ HOOKED | ☐ LONG | ☐ TREE |
| ☐ LONG-THIN | ☐ WIDE | ☐ BUSH |
| ☐ SHORT-POINTED | ☐ THIN | ☐ FEEDER |
| ☐ FLAT-WIDE | ☐ FLUFFY | ☐ FENCE |

COLOURS AND MARKINGS:

| BIRD'S ACTIONS: | DID THE BIRD SING?: ☐ YES  ☐ NO |
|---|---|

### PHOTO/SKETCH

NOTES:

# BIRD WATCHING LOG

| DATE: | TIME: ☐ AM ☐ PM |
|---|---|
| SEASON: | HABITAT: |
| LOCATION: | GPS: |
| WEATHER: | TEMPERATURE: |
| BIRD NAME: | BIRD TYPE: |

| BEAK SHAPE | TAIL | BIRD'S LOCATION |
|---|---|---|
| ☐ CONE | ☐ SHORT | ☐ GROUND |
| ☐ HOOKED | ☐ LONG | ☐ TREE |
| ☐ LONG-THIN | ☐ WIDE | ☐ BUSH |
| ☐ SHORT-POINTED | ☐ THIN | ☐ FEEDER |
| ☐ FLAT-WIDE | ☐ FLUFFY | ☐ FENCE |

COLOURS AND MARKINGS:

| BIRD'S ACTIONS: | DID THE BIRD SING?: ☐ YES ☐ NO |
|---|---|

### PHOTO/SKETCH

NOTES:

# BIRD WATCHING LOG

| DATE: | TIME: ☐ AM ☐ PM |
|---|---|
| SEASON: | HABITAT: |
| LOCATION: | GPS: |
| WEATHER: | TEMPERATURE: |
| BIRD NAME: | BIRD TYPE: |

| BEAK SHAPE | TAIL | BIRD'S LOCATION |
|---|---|---|
| ☐ CONE | ☐ SHORT | ☐ GROUND |
| ☐ HOOKED | ☐ LONG | ☐ TREE |
| ☐ LONG-THIN | ☐ WIDE | ☐ BUSH |
| ☐ SHORT-POINTED | ☐ THIN | ☐ FEEDER |
| ☐ FLAT-WIDE | ☐ FLUFFY | ☐ FENCE |

COLOURS AND MARKINGS:

| BIRD'S ACTIONS: | DID THE BIRD SING?: ☐ YES  ☐ NO |
|---|---|

## PHOTO/SKETCH

NOTES:

# BIRD WATCHING LOG

| DATE: | TIME: ☐ AM ☐ PM |
|---|---|
| SEASON: | HABITAT: |
| LOCATION: | GPS: |
| WEATHER: | TEMPERATURE: |
| BIRD NAME: | BIRD TYPE: |

| BEAK SHAPE | TAIL | BIRD'S LOCATION |
|---|---|---|
| ☐ CONE | ☐ SHORT | ☐ GROUND |
| ☐ HOOKED | ☐ LONG | ☐ TREE |
| ☐ LONG-THIN | ☐ WIDE | ☐ BUSH |
| ☐ SHORT-POINTED | ☐ THIN | ☐ FEEDER |
| ☐ FLAT-WIDE | ☐ FLUFFY | ☐ FENCE |

COLOURS AND MARKINGS:

| BIRD'S ACTIONS: | DID THE BIRD SING?:<br>☐ YES ☐ NO |
|---|---|

## PHOTO/SKETCH

NOTES:

# BIRD WATCHING LOG

| DATE: | TIME: ☐ AM ☐ PM |
|---|---|
| SEASON: | HABITAT: |
| LOCATION: | GPS: |
| WEATHER: | TEMPERATURE: |
| BIRD NAME: | BIRD TYPE: |

| BEAK SHAPE | TAIL | BIRD'S LOCATION |
|---|---|---|
| ☐ CONE | ☐ SHORT | ☐ GROUND |
| ☐ HOOKED | ☐ LONG | ☐ TREE |
| ☐ LONG-THIN | ☐ WIDE | ☐ BUSH |
| ☐ SHORT-POINTED | ☐ THIN | ☐ FEEDER |
| ☐ FLAT-WIDE | ☐ FLUFFY | ☐ FENCE |

COLOURS AND MARKINGS:

| BIRD'S ACTIONS: | DID THE BIRD SING?: ☐ YES  ☐ NO |
|---|---|

## PHOTO/SKETCH

NOTES:

# BIRD WATCHING LOG

| DATE: | TIME: ☐ AM ☐ PM |
|---|---|
| SEASON: | HABITAT: |
| LOCATION: | GPS: |
| WEATHER: | TEMPERATURE: |
| BIRD NAME: | BIRD TYPE: |

| BEAK SHAPE | TAIL | BIRD'S LOCATION |
|---|---|---|
| ☐ CONE | ☐ SHORT | ☐ GROUND |
| ☐ HOOKED | ☐ LONG | ☐ TREE |
| ☐ LONG-THIN | ☐ WIDE | ☐ BUSH |
| ☐ SHORT-POINTED | ☐ THIN | ☐ FEEDER |
| ☐ FLAT-WIDE | ☐ FLUFFY | ☐ FENCE |

COLOURS AND MARKINGS:

| BIRD'S ACTIONS: | DID THE BIRD SING?: ☐ YES ☐ NO |
|---|---|

PHOTO/SKETCH

NOTES:

# BIRD WATCHING LOG

| DATE: | TIME: ☐ AM ☐ PM |
|---|---|
| SEASON: | HABITAT: |
| LOCATION: | GPS: |
| WEATHER: | TEMPERATURE: |
| BIRD NAME: | BIRD TYPE: |

| BEAK SHAPE | TAIL | BIRD'S LOCATION |
|---|---|---|
| ☐ CONE | ☐ SHORT | ☐ GROUND |
| ☐ HOOKED | ☐ LONG | ☐ TREE |
| ☐ LONG-THIN | ☐ WIDE | ☐ BUSH |
| ☐ SHORT-POINTED | ☐ THIN | ☐ FEEDER |
| ☐ FLAT-WIDE | ☐ FLUFFY | ☐ FENCE |

COLOURS AND MARKINGS:

| BIRD'S ACTIONS: | DID THE BIRD SING?<br>☐ YES   ☐ NO |
|---|---|

## PHOTO/SKETCH

NOTES:

# BIRD WATCHING LOG

| DATE: | TIME: ☐ AM ☐ PM |
|---|---|
| SEASON: | HABITAT: |
| LOCATION: | GPS: |
| WEATHER: | TEMPERATURE: |
| BIRD NAME: | BIRD TYPE: |

| BEAK SHAPE | TAIL | BIRD'S LOCATION |
|---|---|---|
| ☐ CONE | ☐ SHORT | ☐ GROUND |
| ☐ HOOKED | ☐ LONG | ☐ TREE |
| ☐ LONG-THIN | ☐ WIDE | ☐ BUSH |
| ☐ SHORT-POINTED | ☐ THIN | ☐ FEEDER |
| ☐ FLAT-WIDE | ☐ FLUFFY | ☐ FENCE |

COLOURS AND MARKINGS:

| BIRD'S ACTIONS: | DID THE BIRD SING?: ☐ YES  ☐ NO |
|---|---|

## PHOTO/SKETCH

NOTES:

# BIRD WATCHING LOG

| | |
|---|---|
| DATE: | TIME: ☐ AM ☐ PM |
| SEASON: | HABITAT: |
| LOCATION: | GPS: |
| WEATHER: | TEMPERATURE: |
| BIRD NAME: | BIRD TYPE: |

### BEAK SHAPE
- ☐ CONE
- ☐ HOOKED
- ☐ LONG-THIN
- ☐ SHORT-POINTED
- ☐ FLAT-WIDE

### TAIL
- ☐ SHORT
- ☐ LONG
- ☐ WIDE
- ☐ THIN
- ☐ FLUFFY

### BIRD'S LOCATION
- ☐ GROUND
- ☐ TREE
- ☐ BUSH
- ☐ FEEDER
- ☐ FENCE

COLOURS AND MARKINGS:

BIRD'S ACTIONS:

DID THE BIRD SING?:
☐ YES    ☐ NO

### PHOTO/SKETCH

NOTES:

# BIRD WATCHING LOG

| | |
|---|---|
| DATE: | TIME: ☐ AM ☐ PM |
| SEASON: | HABITAT: |
| LOCATION: | GPS: |
| WEATHER: | TEMPERATURE: |
| BIRD NAME: | BIRD TYPE: |

| BEAK SHAPE | TAIL | BIRD'S LOCATION |
|---|---|---|
| ☐ CONE | ☐ SHORT | ☐ GROUND |
| ☐ HOOKED | ☐ LONG | ☐ TREE |
| ☐ LONG-THIN | ☐ WIDE | ☐ BUSH |
| ☐ SHORT-POINTED | ☐ THIN | ☐ FEEDER |
| ☐ FLAT-WIDE | ☐ FLUFFY | ☐ FENCE |

COLOURS AND MARKINGS:

BIRD'S ACTIONS:

DID THE BIRD SING?:
☐ YES     ☐ NO

PHOTO/SKETCH

NOTES:

# BIRD WATCHING LOG

| DATE: | TIME: ☐ AM ☐ PM |
|---|---|
| SEASON: | HABITAT: |
| LOCATION: | GPS: |
| WEATHER: | TEMPERATURE: |
| BIRD NAME: | BIRD TYPE: |

| BEAK SHAPE | TAIL | BIRD'S LOCATION |
|---|---|---|
| ☐ CONE | ☐ SHORT | ☐ GROUND |
| ☐ HOOKED | ☐ LONG | ☐ TREE |
| ☐ LONG-THIN | ☐ WIDE | ☐ BUSH |
| ☐ SHORT-POINTED | ☐ THIN | ☐ FEEDER |
| ☐ FLAT-WIDE | ☐ FLUFFY | ☐ FENCE |

COLOURS AND MARKINGS:

| BIRD'S ACTIONS: | DID THE BIRD SING?: ☐ YES   ☐ NO |
|---|---|

### PHOTO/SKETCH

NOTES:

# BIRD WATCHING LOG

| DATE: | TIME: ☐ AM ☐ PM |
|---|---|
| SEASON: | HABITAT: |
| LOCATION: | GPS: |
| WEATHER: | TEMPERATURE: |
| BIRD NAME: | BIRD TYPE: |

| BEAK SHAPE | TAIL | BIRD'S LOCATION |
|---|---|---|
| ☐ CONE | ☐ SHORT | ☐ GROUND |
| ☐ HOOKED | ☐ LONG | ☐ TREE |
| ☐ LONG-THIN | ☐ WIDE | ☐ BUSH |
| ☐ SHORT-POINTED | ☐ THIN | ☐ FEEDER |
| ☐ FLAT-WIDE | ☐ FLUFFY | ☐ FENCE |

COLOURS AND MARKINGS:

| BIRD'S ACTIONS: | DID THE BIRD SING?: ☐ YES ☐ NO |
|---|---|

PHOTO/SKETCH

NOTES:

# BIRD WATCHING LOG

| DATE: | TIME: ☐ AM ☐ PM |
|---|---|
| SEASON: | HABITAT: |
| LOCATION: | GPS: |
| WEATHER: | TEMPERATURE: |
| BIRD NAME: | BIRD TYPE: |

| BEAK SHAPE | TAIL | BIRD'S LOCATION |
|---|---|---|
| ☐ CONE | ☐ SHORT | ☐ GROUND |
| ☐ HOOKED | ☐ LONG | ☐ TREE |
| ☐ LONG-THIN | ☐ WIDE | ☐ BUSH |
| ☐ SHORT-POINTED | ☐ THIN | ☐ FEEDER |
| ☐ FLAT-WIDE | ☐ FLUFFY | ☐ FENCE |

COLOURS AND MARKINGS:

| BIRD'S ACTIONS: | DID THE BIRD SING?: ☐ YES ☐ NO |
|---|---|

## PHOTO/SKETCH

NOTES:

# BIRD WATCHING LOG

| | |
|---|---|
| DATE: | TIME: ☐ AM ☐ PM |
| SEASON: | HABITAT: |
| LOCATION: | GPS: |
| WEATHER: | TEMPERATURE: |
| BIRD NAME: | BIRD TYPE: |

| BEAK SHAPE | TAIL | BIRD'S LOCATION |
|---|---|---|
| ☐ CONE | ☐ SHORT | ☐ GROUND |
| ☐ HOOKED | ☐ LONG | ☐ TREE |
| ☐ LONG-THIN | ☐ WIDE | ☐ BUSH |
| ☐ SHORT-POINTED | ☐ THIN | ☐ FEEDER |
| ☐ FLAT-WIDE | ☐ FLUFFY | ☐ FENCE |

COLOURS AND MARKINGS:

| BIRD'S ACTIONS: | DID THE BIRD SING?:<br>☐ YES   ☐ NO |
|---|---|

### PHOTO/SKETCH

NOTES:

# BIRD WATCHING LOG

| | |
|---|---|
| DATE: | TIME:  ☐ AM ☐ PM |
| SEASON: | HABITAT: |
| LOCATION: | GPS: |
| WEATHER: | TEMPERATURE: |
| BIRD NAME: | BIRD TYPE: |

| BEAK SHAPE | TAIL | BIRD'S LOCATION |
|---|---|---|
| ☐ CONE | ☐ SHORT | ☐ GROUND |
| ☐ HOOKED | ☐ LONG | ☐ TREE |
| ☐ LONG-THIN | ☐ WIDE | ☐ BUSH |
| ☐ SHORT-POINTED | ☐ THIN | ☐ FEEDER |
| ☐ FLAT-WIDE | ☐ FLUFFY | ☐ FENCE |

COLOURS AND MARKINGS:

| BIRD'S ACTIONS: | DID THE BIRD SING?:<br>☐ YES    ☐ NO |
|---|---|

### PHOTO/SKETCH

NOTES:

# BIRD WATCHING LOG

| | |
|---|---|
| DATE: | TIME: ☐ AM ☐ PM |
| SEASON: | HABITAT: |
| LOCATION: | GPS: |
| WEATHER: | TEMPERATURE: |
| BIRD NAME: | BIRD TYPE: |

| BEAK SHAPE | TAIL | BIRD'S LOCATION |
|---|---|---|
| ☐ CONE | ☐ SHORT | ☐ GROUND |
| ☐ HOOKED | ☐ LONG | ☐ TREE |
| ☐ LONG-THIN | ☐ WIDE | ☐ BUSH |
| ☐ SHORT-POINTED | ☐ THIN | ☐ FEEDER |
| ☐ FLAT-WIDE | ☐ FLUFFY | ☐ FENCE |

COLOURS AND MARKINGS:

BIRD'S ACTIONS:

DID THE BIRD SING?:
☐ YES    ☐ NO

## PHOTO/SKETCH

NOTES:

# BIRD WATCHING LOG

| DATE: | TIME: ☐ AM ☐ PM |
|---|---|
| SEASON: | HABITAT: |
| LOCATION: | GPS: |
| WEATHER: | TEMPERATURE: |
| BIRD NAME: | BIRD TYPE: |

| BEAK SHAPE | TAIL | BIRD'S LOCATION |
|---|---|---|
| ☐ CONE | ☐ SHORT | ☐ GROUND |
| ☐ HOOKED | ☐ LONG | ☐ TREE |
| ☐ LONG-THIN | ☐ WIDE | ☐ BUSH |
| ☐ SHORT-POINTED | ☐ THIN | ☐ FEEDER |
| ☐ FLAT-WIDE | ☐ FLUFFY | ☐ FENCE |

COLOURS AND MARKINGS:

| BIRD'S ACTIONS: | DID THE BIRD SING?: ☐ YES ☐ NO |
|---|---|

## PHOTO/SKETCH

NOTES:

# BIRD WATCHING LOG

| | |
|---|---|
| DATE: | TIME: ☐ AM ☐ PM |
| SEASON: | HABITAT: |
| LOCATION: | GPS: |
| WEATHER: | TEMPERATURE: |
| BIRD NAME: | BIRD TYPE: |

| BEAK SHAPE | TAIL | BIRD'S LOCATION |
|---|---|---|
| ☐ CONE | ☐ SHORT | ☐ GROUND |
| ☐ HOOKED | ☐ LONG | ☐ TREE |
| ☐ LONG-THIN | ☐ WIDE | ☐ BUSH |
| ☐ SHORT-POINTED | ☐ THIN | ☐ FEEDER |
| ☐ FLAT-WIDE | ☐ FLUFFY | ☐ FENCE |

COLOURS AND MARKINGS:

| BIRD'S ACTIONS: | DID THE BIRD SING?: <br> ☐ YES   ☐ NO |
|---|---|

## PHOTO/SKETCH

NOTES:

# BIRD WATCHING LOG

| DATE: | TIME: ☐ AM ☐ PM |
|---|---|
| SEASON: | HABITAT: |
| LOCATION: | GPS: |
| WEATHER: | TEMPERATURE: |
| BIRD NAME: | BIRD TYPE: |

| BEAK SHAPE | TAIL | BIRD'S LOCATION |
|---|---|---|
| ☐ CONE | ☐ SHORT | ☐ GROUND |
| ☐ HOOKED | ☐ LONG | ☐ TREE |
| ☐ LONG-THIN | ☐ WIDE | ☐ BUSH |
| ☐ SHORT-POINTED | ☐ THIN | ☐ FEEDER |
| ☐ FLAT-WIDE | ☐ FLUFFY | ☐ FENCE |

COLOURS AND MARKINGS:

| BIRD'S ACTIONS: | DID THE BIRD SING?: ☐ YES ☐ NO |
|---|---|

## PHOTO/SKETCH

NOTES:

# BIRD WATCHING LOG

| | |
|---|---|
| DATE: | TIME: ☐ AM ☐ PM |
| SEASON: | HABITAT: |
| LOCATION: | GPS: |
| WEATHER: | TEMPERATURE: |
| BIRD NAME: | BIRD TYPE: |

| BEAK SHAPE | TAIL | BIRD'S LOCATION |
|---|---|---|
| ☐ CONE | ☐ SHORT | ☐ GROUND |
| ☐ HOOKED | ☐ LONG | ☐ TREE |
| ☐ LONG-THIN | ☐ WIDE | ☐ BUSH |
| ☐ SHORT-POINTED | ☐ THIN | ☐ FEEDER |
| ☐ FLAT-WIDE | ☐ FLUFFY | ☐ FENCE |

COLOURS AND MARKINGS:

| BIRD'S ACTIONS: | DID THE BIRD SING?:<br>☐ YES  ☐ NO |
|---|---|

## PHOTO/SKETCH

NOTES:

# BIRD WATCHING LOG

| DATE: | TIME: ☐ AM ☐ PM |
|---|---|
| SEASON: | HABITAT: |
| LOCATION: | GPS: |
| WEATHER: | TEMPERATURE: |
| BIRD NAME: | BIRD TYPE: |

| BEAK SHAPE | TAIL | BIRD'S LOCATION |
|---|---|---|
| ☐ CONE | ☐ SHORT | ☐ GROUND |
| ☐ HOOKED | ☐ LONG | ☐ TREE |
| ☐ LONG-THIN | ☐ WIDE | ☐ BUSH |
| ☐ SHORT-POINTED | ☐ THIN | ☐ FEEDER |
| ☐ FLAT-WIDE | ☐ FLUFFY | ☐ FENCE |

COLOURS AND MARKINGS:

| BIRD'S ACTIONS: | DID THE BIRD SING?: ☐ YES    ☐ NO |
|---|---|

### PHOTO/SKETCH

NOTES:

# BIRD WATCHING LOG

| DATE: | TIME: ☐ AM ☐ PM |
|---|---|
| SEASON: | HABITAT: |
| LOCATION: | GPS: |
| WEATHER: | TEMPERATURE: |
| BIRD NAME: | BIRD TYPE: |

| BEAK SHAPE | TAIL | BIRD'S LOCATION |
|---|---|---|
| ☐ CONE | ☐ SHORT | ☐ GROUND |
| ☐ HOOKED | ☐ LONG | ☐ TREE |
| ☐ LONG-THIN | ☐ WIDE | ☐ BUSH |
| ☐ SHORT-POINTED | ☐ THIN | ☐ FEEDER |
| ☐ FLAT-WIDE | ☐ FLUFFY | ☐ FENCE |

COLOURS AND MARKINGS:

| BIRD'S ACTIONS: | DID THE BIRD SING?: ☐ YES ☐ NO |
|---|---|

## PHOTO/SKETCH

NOTES:

# BIRD WATCHING LOG

| DATE: | TIME: ☐ AM ☐ PM |
|---|---|
| SEASON: | HABITAT: |
| LOCATION: | GPS: |
| WEATHER: | TEMPERATURE: |
| BIRD NAME: | BIRD TYPE: |

| BEAK SHAPE | TAIL | BIRD'S LOCATION |
|---|---|---|
| ☐ CONE | ☐ SHORT | ☐ GROUND |
| ☐ HOOKED | ☐ LONG | ☐ TREE |
| ☐ LONG-THIN | ☐ WIDE | ☐ BUSH |
| ☐ SHORT-POINTED | ☐ THIN | ☐ FEEDER |
| ☐ FLAT-WIDE | ☐ FLUFFY | ☐ FENCE |

COLOURS AND MARKINGS:

| BIRD'S ACTIONS: | DID THE BIRD SING?:<br>☐ YES  ☐ NO |
|---|---|

## PHOTO/SKETCH

NOTES:

# BIRD WATCHING LOG

| DATE: | TIME: ☐ AM ☐ PM |
|---|---|
| SEASON: | HABITAT: |
| LOCATION: | GPS: |
| WEATHER: | TEMPERATURE: |
| BIRD NAME: | BIRD TYPE: |

| BEAK SHAPE | TAIL | BIRD'S LOCATION |
|---|---|---|
| ☐ CONE | ☐ SHORT | ☐ GROUND |
| ☐ HOOKED | ☐ LONG | ☐ TREE |
| ☐ LONG-THIN | ☐ WIDE | ☐ BUSH |
| ☐ SHORT-POINTED | ☐ THIN | ☐ FEEDER |
| ☐ FLAT-WIDE | ☐ FLUFFY | ☐ FENCE |

COLOURS AND MARKINGS:

| BIRD'S ACTIONS: | DID THE BIRD SING?: ☐ YES  ☐ NO |
|---|---|

### PHOTO/SKETCH

NOTES:

# BIRD WATCHING LOG

| DATE: | TIME: ☐ AM ☐ PM |
|---|---|
| SEASON: | HABITAT: |
| LOCATION: | GPS: |
| WEATHER: | TEMPERATURE: |
| BIRD NAME: | BIRD TYPE: |

| BEAK SHAPE | TAIL | BIRD'S LOCATION |
|---|---|---|
| ☐ CONE | ☐ SHORT | ☐ GROUND |
| ☐ HOOKED | ☐ LONG | ☐ TREE |
| ☐ LONG-THIN | ☐ WIDE | ☐ BUSH |
| ☐ SHORT-POINTED | ☐ THIN | ☐ FEEDER |
| ☐ FLAT-WIDE | ☐ FLUFFY | ☐ FENCE |

COLOURS AND MARKINGS:

| BIRD'S ACTIONS: | DID THE BIRD SING?:<br>☐ YES  ☐ NO |
|---|---|

## PHOTO/SKETCH

NOTES:

# BIRD WATCHING LOG

| | |
|---|---|
| DATE: | TIME: ☐ AM ☐ PM |
| SEASON: | HABITAT: |
| LOCATION: | GPS: |
| WEATHER: | TEMPERATURE: |
| BIRD NAME: | BIRD TYPE: |

| BEAK SHAPE | TAIL | BIRD'S LOCATION |
|---|---|---|
| ☐ CONE | ☐ SHORT | ☐ GROUND |
| ☐ HOOKED | ☐ LONG | ☐ TREE |
| ☐ LONG-THIN | ☐ WIDE | ☐ BUSH |
| ☐ SHORT-POINTED | ☐ THIN | ☐ FEEDER |
| ☐ FLAT-WIDE | ☐ FLUFFY | ☐ FENCE |

COLOURS AND MARKINGS:

| BIRD'S ACTIONS: | DID THE BIRD SING?: ☐ YES  ☐ NO |
|---|---|

## PHOTO/SKETCH

NOTES:

# BIRD WATCHING LOG

| | |
|---|---|
| DATE: | TIME: ☐ AM ☐ PM |
| SEASON: | HABITAT: |
| LOCATION: | GPS: |
| WEATHER: | TEMPERATURE: |
| BIRD NAME: | BIRD TYPE: |

## BEAK SHAPE

- ☐ CONE
- ☐ HOOKED
- ☐ LONG-THIN
- ☐ SHORT-POINTED
- ☐ FLAT-WIDE

## TAIL

- ☐ SHORT
- ☐ LONG
- ☐ WIDE
- ☐ THIN
- ☐ FLUFFY

## BIRD'S LOCATION

- ☐ GROUND
- ☐ TREE
- ☐ BUSH
- ☐ FEEDER
- ☐ FENCE

COLOURS AND MARKINGS:

BIRD'S ACTIONS:

DID THE BIRD SING?:
☐ YES   ☐ NO

## PHOTO/SKETCH

NOTES:

# BIRD WATCHING LOG

| DATE: | TIME: ☐ AM ☐ PM |
|---|---|
| SEASON: | HABITAT: |
| LOCATION: | GPS: |
| WEATHER: | TEMPERATURE: |
| BIRD NAME: | BIRD TYPE: |

| BEAK SHAPE | TAIL | BIRD'S LOCATION |
|---|---|---|
| ☐ CONE | ☐ SHORT | ☐ GROUND |
| ☐ HOOKED | ☐ LONG | ☐ TREE |
| ☐ LONG-THIN | ☐ WIDE | ☐ BUSH |
| ☐ SHORT-POINTED | ☐ THIN | ☐ FEEDER |
| ☐ FLAT-WIDE | ☐ FLUFFY | ☐ FENCE |

COLOURS AND MARKINGS:

| BIRD'S ACTIONS: | DID THE BIRD SING?: ☐ YES ☐ NO |
|---|---|

## PHOTO/SKETCH

NOTES:

# BIRD WATCHING LOG

| DATE: | TIME: ☐ AM ☐ PM |
|---|---|
| SEASON: | HABITAT: |
| LOCATION: | GPS: |
| WEATHER: | TEMPERATURE: |
| BIRD NAME: | BIRD TYPE: |

| BEAK SHAPE | TAIL | BIRD'S LOCATION |
|---|---|---|
| ☐ CONE | ☐ SHORT | ☐ GROUND |
| ☐ HOOKED | ☐ LONG | ☐ TREE |
| ☐ LONG-THIN | ☐ WIDE | ☐ BUSH |
| ☐ SHORT-POINTED | ☐ THIN | ☐ FEEDER |
| ☐ FLAT-WIDE | ☐ FLUFFY | ☐ FENCE |

COLOURS AND MARKINGS:

| BIRD'S ACTIONS: | DID THE BIRD SING?:<br>☐ YES ☐ NO |
|---|---|

### PHOTO/SKETCH

NOTES:

# BIRD WATCHING LOG

| DATE: | TIME: ☐ AM ☐ PM |
|---|---|
| SEASON: | HABITAT: |
| LOCATION: | GPS: |
| WEATHER: | TEMPERATURE: |
| BIRD NAME: | BIRD TYPE: |

| BEAK SHAPE | TAIL | BIRD'S LOCATION |
|---|---|---|
| ☐ CONE | ☐ SHORT | ☐ GROUND |
| ☐ HOOKED | ☐ LONG | ☐ TREE |
| ☐ LONG-THIN | ☐ WIDE | ☐ BUSH |
| ☐ SHORT-POINTED | ☐ THIN | ☐ FEEDER |
| ☐ FLAT-WIDE | ☐ FLUFFY | ☐ FENCE |

COLOURS AND MARKINGS:

| BIRD'S ACTIONS: | DID THE BIRD SING?: ☐ YES   ☐ NO |
|---|---|

### PHOTO/SKETCH

NOTES:

# BIRD WATCHING LOG

| | |
|---|---|
| DATE: | TIME: ☐ AM ☐ PM |
| SEASON: | HABITAT: |
| LOCATION: | GPS: |
| WEATHER: | TEMPERATURE: |
| BIRD NAME: | BIRD TYPE: |

| BEAK SHAPE | TAIL | BIRD'S LOCATION |
|---|---|---|
| ☐ CONE | ☐ SHORT | ☐ GROUND |
| ☐ HOOKED | ☐ LONG | ☐ TREE |
| ☐ LONG-THIN | ☐ WIDE | ☐ BUSH |
| ☐ SHORT-POINTED | ☐ THIN | ☐ FEEDER |
| ☐ FLAT-WIDE | ☐ FLUFFY | ☐ FENCE |

COLOURS AND MARKINGS:

| BIRD'S ACTIONS: | DID THE BIRD SING?: ☐ YES ☐ NO |
|---|---|

## PHOTO/SKETCH

NOTES:

# BIRD WATCHING LOG

| | |
|---|---|
| DATE: | TIME: ☐ AM ☐ PM |
| SEASON: | HABITAT: |
| LOCATION: | GPS: |
| WEATHER: | TEMPERATURE: |
| BIRD NAME: | BIRD TYPE: |

| BEAK SHAPE | TAIL | BIRD'S LOCATION |
|---|---|---|
| ☐ CONE | ☐ SHORT | ☐ GROUND |
| ☐ HOOKED | ☐ LONG | ☐ TREE |
| ☐ LONG-THIN | ☐ WIDE | ☐ BUSH |
| ☐ SHORT-POINTED | ☐ THIN | ☐ FEEDER |
| ☐ FLAT-WIDE | ☐ FLUFFY | ☐ FENCE |

COLOURS AND MARKINGS:

| BIRD'S ACTIONS: | DID THE BIRD SING?:<br>☐ YES    ☐ NO |
|---|---|

### PHOTO/SKETCH

NOTES:

# BIRD WATCHING LOG

| | |
|---|---|
| DATE: | TIME: ☐ AM ☐ PM |
| SEASON: | HABITAT: |
| LOCATION: | GPS: |
| WEATHER: | TEMPERATURE: |
| BIRD NAME: | BIRD TYPE: |

| BEAK SHAPE | TAIL | BIRD'S LOCATION |
|---|---|---|
| ☐ CONE | ☐ SHORT | ☐ GROUND |
| ☐ HOOKED | ☐ LONG | ☐ TREE |
| ☐ LONG-THIN | ☐ WIDE | ☐ BUSH |
| ☐ SHORT-POINTED | ☐ THIN | ☐ FEEDER |
| ☐ FLAT-WIDE | ☐ FLUFFY | ☐ FENCE |

COLOURS AND MARKINGS:

| BIRD'S ACTIONS: | DID THE BIRD SING?: ☐ YES   ☐ NO |
|---|---|

## PHOTO/SKETCH

NOTES: